Praise for Iris Origo

WAR IN VAL D'ORCIA

'A remarkable war diary' *Daily Telegraph*

'A remarkably moving document that, like the best
of the elemental war stories, eventually becomes a
statement about the unplanned nature and folly of war'
New York Times

'Iris is unsparing in offering her readers her own keen
and compassionate observations of the world around
her, investing it at times with a startling immediacy'
Virginia Nicholson

'It is jolting to recall, through Origo's sober and
self-effacing prose, the atrocious conditions of the
summer of 1944' *FT*

'Relates in vivid detail the experiences of civilians who
had the terrible misfortune to find themselves pinned
between battling armies ... beyond doubt a minor
masterpiece' *Washington Post*

IMAGES AND SHADOWS

'An elegiac biography ... illuminating' *Daily Telegraph*

'Elegant and intelligent' *Spectator*

'A wonderful writer ... *Images and Shadows* is as delicious and tear-inducing as Downton Abbey' *New York Times*

A STUDY IN SOLITUDE

'Sympathetic and discerning ... the ideal biographer' *Spectator*

'Origo evokes the bittersweet, unlived life with ... sympathy and clarity' *Publisher's Weekly*

THE LAST ATTACHMENT

'A sublime wordsmith and an astute and passionate observer of human behavior' *New York Times*

'A fascinating and sincere biography ... a treasure trove ... gives off a rich aroma of those fargone and unbelievably romantic days' *Kirkus*

'A fascinating book ... an exciting and complex story admirably told' Clive Bell, *Spectator*

A CHILL
IN THE AIR

An Italian War Diary 1939–1940

Iris Origo

Introduction by Lucy Hughes-Hallett

With an afterword by Katia Lysy

PUSHKIN PRESS
LONDON

Pushkin Press
71–75 Shelton Street
London, WC2H 9JQ

A Chill in the Air was first published in Great Britain
by Pushkin Press in 2017

1 3 5 7 9 8 6 4 2

ISBN 978 1 78227 355 4

Designed and typeset by MRules, London

Printed and bound by CPI Group (UK) Ltd, Croydon, CR0 4YY

www.pushkinpress.com

Contents

Introduction

In her late sixties Iris Origo wrote a memoir. In looking back on her life as a writer she devoted several
pages to each of her biographies (Leopardi, Byron's
daughter Allegra and his mistress Teresa Guiccioli, St
Bernardino) but only one subordinate clause to "my
little war diary". That "little" diary, first published in
1947 as *War in Val d'Orcia*, is the most admired of her
books. Now here is another of her diaries – published
for the first time – one that shows a rather different
Origo, and describes with vivid clarity the strange
period – the months leading up to Italy's entry into
the Second World War – when Italians lived in suspense, waiting to know whether they were going
to be called upon to kill and be killed alongside the
Germans, whom the majority of them detested, in
what Churchill was to call the "unnecessary war".

When it came out in 1947, *War in Val d'Orcia* was an immediate success. Origo was praised for her spare, elegant prose and the trenchancy of her thinking. Reviewers like Elizabeth Bowen and L.P. Hartley welcomed her into the ranks of first-rate writers. More – the book had a significant effect on Anglo-Italian relations. While the Allies were bombing German-held Italian cities, Origo and her Italian husband Antonio, and the people on their estate, hid and fed partisans and fugitive British soldiers, and helped the latter on their way southwards to join the advancing Allied armies. They risked summary execution by the German occupiers. As Origo's biographer Caroline Moorehead writes, "Sometimes, as Iris was talking to partisans or escaped prisoners of war in the garden, giving them maps and food, Antonio would be tying up a German patrol in conversation at the front of the house." Repeatedly the couple, out of decency, kindness, and a sense of the responsibilities attendant on their privileged position, imperilled themselves. The Italian peasants who worked on their estate did too, sharing their meagre supplies and risking their lives. The world took note. As *La Stampa*'s reviewer wrote, "*War in Val d'Orcia* has done us more good than a battle won by our side."

It had shown the English-speaking world how self-less and how brave Italians could be. It also made Iris Origo into a celebrated author, and a heroine as well. When German troops turned her, her family, and their many helpless protégés off their estate, she led a troop of children, women with babies, and infirm old people in a hair-raising march across countryside that was being shelled from the air by the Allies. After several hours they reached the foot of the hill on which Montepulciano sits, and halted briefly to gather strength before the steep climb up to the town where they hoped to find a refuge.

> As we sat there, a little group of citizens appeared, then yet another: they had seen us from the ramparts, and were coming down to meet us with open arms. Many of them were partisans; others were refugees whom we had helped. They shouldered the children and our packages, and in a triumphant procession, cheered by so much kindness, we climbed up the village street, Antonio at the head, with Donata [their baby] on his shoulder.

Afterwards she wrote, "Never was there a more touching welcome."

The story of Iris Origo, the foreign Marchesa who was so brave and so generous to the people of her adopted country, was given a commensurately warm welcome by readers all over the English-speaking world.

*

That story is true, but it shows only one aspect of the colourful life and complex personality of Iris Origo. In wartime she was a kind of Mother Courage, but she was also a sophisticated and cosmopolitan woman with a fierce intellect. The diarist Frances Partridge met her when she was a twenty-one-year-old bride, "so slight, like a flame, very delicate, almost like a Botticelli, with a very quick voice and a mind as quick, running from one thing to another, and alarming because so clever". A few years later, in 1935, Origo was in London again with her beau of the moment, the novelist Leo Myers, and there she met Virginia Woolf. Woolf describes her. "She is tremulous, nervous – very – stammers a little... but honest eyed; very blue eyed. She's clean and picks her feet up." First impressions were good enough for the Woolfs to invite Origo to dinner and Virginia again noted that Iris was "honest", "genuine", as well as being "intelligent". She had these sterling qualities, and she glittered as well. She was very well connected and very well dressed. "I like her Bird of Paradise flight through the gay world," wrote Woolf . "A long green feather in her hat." Another friend wrote, "It was impossible not to be excited by Iris... She was technically on fire."

*

This vivid bird of passage had led a cosmopolitan and privileged life. Her mother, Sybil, was the daughter of the Anglo-Irish peer the Earl of Desart. Her father's family were rich Americans. Their fortune came from railroads, shipping and sugar-beet. They spent it on philanthropy, on being among the founders of the New York Public Library, on their houses on Madison Avenue and Long Island and a box at the Metropolitan opera. Moving from one grand family home to another, Iris grew up knowing she was, in many ways, exceptionally fortunate.

No amount of money or social position, though, could protect her from loss. Within weeks of her birth her father, Bayard Cutting, had his first haemorrhage. Throughout her early childhood Iris and her parents traversed the globe in search of treatment for his tuberculosis or, failing that, at least a climate that might alleviate it. They tried California; they tried Switzerland; they tried various Italian resorts by the sea or in the mountains. They were in Egypt when, just short of his thirtieth birthday, he died. Iris, whom he dotingly called "Bullet-head" or "Fatty", was seven. Sixty years later she wrote that her father's death was one of the two most significant events of her life, and that "there is no greater grief than that of parting".

Before he died, Bayard had made plans for her. His last letter to Sibyl alludes to the objections his family had made to his marrying an Englishwoman, and goes on to say he wants Iris to grow up "free from all this national feeling which makes people so unhappy. Bring her up somewhere where she does not belong, then she can't have it". Italy, he suggested, would be best. There she could become "cosmopolitan, deep down" and, when the time came, "be free to love and marry anyone she likes, of any country, without its being difficult". Sibyl complied. Bayard had left her rich. She rented (and subsequently bought) the Villa Medici, in the hills above Florence, and there, in a house built by Michelozzo for Cosimo di Medici, and described by Vasari as "a magnificent and noble palace", Iris grew up.

As the only child of an eccentric and hypochondriac

mother she didn't have the easiest adolescence, but it was a mind-broadening one. Her mother, reclining on a sofa in a Fortuny tea-gown, would read poetry aloud to her or, when feeling more energetic, would drag her along on excursions around Italy, barging uninvited into private houses while teenaged Iris cringed with embarrassment. In Fiesole, the social life of the then numerous English colony was busy: Bernard and Mary Berenson were among the neighbours with whom Sybil played at "conoshing", an art-historical guessing game in which participants vied in displaying their connoisseurship. For these people, wrote Iris later, the First World War "was only a distant rumble, an inconvenient and unpleasant noise offstage". Ignoring it, Sybil improved the garden and shopped indefatigably at the *antiquari* of Florence. At Iris's coming-out ball, "the terrace, where supper was laid on little tables, was lit with Japanese lanterns; the fireflies darted among the wheat in the *podere* below; the air was heavy with jasmine and roses, and at midnight fireworks from the west terrace soared like jewelled fountains between us and the valley".

The young woman who emerged from t' ~arefied atmosphere, in which high-mindedness ∂ were so curiously blended – couldn't w∂

She wanted to go to Oxford (she had, unusually for a girl, been given a classical education) but she was persuaded instead to be a debutante three times over. After Florence came England, where she enjoyed the "wild gallop" at the end of a hunt ball, but where she felt as out of place as "a Pekinese in a pack of hounds". In New York she was dismayed by the "stag line" of college boys, swigging poisonous hooch from hip-flasks (these were the Prohibition years) and becomingly predictably boorish as a result. No wonder, back in Florence, she fell for Antonio Origo. Her mother thought he was too grown-up (he was ten years older than Iris) and too good-looking. Sibyl repeatedly postponed the wedding by taking to her bed with mysterious complaints until the family doctor "bluntly" told Iris to go ahead regardless: "if we didn't get married at once we never would". And so they did, in the Villa Medici's chapel, in 1924.

Antonio's father was a sculptor and a close friend of the poet Gabriele d'Annunzio, but until the war interrupted his career, Antonio was being groomed to become a businessman. Together with Iris, though, he determined on a different course. Each of the young people had money; Iris's father had left her enough to make her independent. Rebelling against their families' plans for them, the couple sought out and bought the estate of La Foce in southern Tuscany, choosing it, against all advice, precisely because the land was so eroded and harsh, the buildings so dilapidated, water so scarce and the navigable roads non-existent. They were looking for "a place with enough work to fill our lifetimes". Iris had hoped as well for "some beauty" but La Foce, when they found it, was a "a lunar landscape, pale and inhuman" with the "bleakness of a desert". The main house was dark, with no electric light, no heating, no garden (because there was only just enough well-water for necessities) and no bathroom. Undaunted, they bought it, determined to "turn this bare clay into wheat fields, to rebuild these farms and see prosperity return to their inhabitants, to restore the greenness of these mutilated woods". Quite an undertaking. The estate included twenty-five farms. Iris was still only twenty-two.

*

When she fell in love with Antonio Origo, Iris chose not only a man but a nation. She continued to visit her relations in England and America. She loved travelling, and every year, even after her adored son Gianni was born, she was often away on jaunts abroad. But she was tied to an expanse of Italian land. In the early 1930s she wavered – spending longish periods in England and indulging in a couple of love-affairs. But by the time the Second World War was imminent, she was back at La Foce, committed with all her heart to her home, to her marriage and to her life in Italy. Her distress when she found her adopted country at war with both her native ones was great, but she met it with characteristic poise. "I decided that, for the time being, all that was required of me was to try to keep as steady as possible." As an aid to that steadiness she thought, "Perhaps it might be useful to try to clear my mind by setting down, as truthfully and simply as I can, the tiny facet of the world's events which I myself, in the months ahead, shall encounter at first hand." *A Chill in the Air* is the diary she wrote as the outcome of that decision.

*

Nowadays the word "Fascist" is used as a catch-all pejorative term. It is disconcerting to read someone like Origo – a liberal internationalist – remarking, for instance, that it was her "good fortune" to be a landowner under the Fascist regime, when Mussolini's "Battle of the Wheat" meant that landowners were encouraged, and generously subsidised, to improve their land. In her opinion, Fascist *consorzi* – landowners' associations – like the one of which Antonio became the president, "represented what was best in the Fascist regime". Iris praises some of their leading lights, like the "man of outstanding ability and charm" who combined an "uncritical acceptance of Fascist slogans" with admirable enthusiasm for their work. To read her memoirs and diaries is to be obliged to lay aside simplistic judgements and to remember that, for a full generation, Italians of all temperaments and shades of opinion got by – reluctantly, contentedly or, in most cases, just pragmatically – under Fascist rule.

Origo (like many British observers, including Churchill) was impressed by the Duce. "My dear," she wrote to a friend in 1930, "Mussolini is a very great man." She saw in him "firmness... and a sense of complete remoteness and loneliness. Here was someone on a larger scale than most people". Later her views shifted. In the late thirties she became close to the Bracci family and the group of courageous anti-Fascists around them. For many years, though, she – ostensibly anyway – closed her eyes to the oppressiveness of the totalitarian regime. In her memoirs she was to acknowledge a "disinclination to write about the long years of Fascism, during which I learned to hold my tongue and preserve my convictions". She was an outsider – a foreigner – trying to fit in. Besides, she wrote, "I doubt whether there is much to be gained by dwelling on those periods of one's life of which the dominant flavour, in recollection, is distaste." That reticence, though, came with hindsight, and was for public consumption. *A Chill in the Air* – written with the urgency of immediate observation and not intended for publication – shows an energetic, mature woman (she was thirty-seven), full of forthright opinions and lively interest in the tremendous events going on around her.

*

She was exceptionally well connected. Her godfather William Phillips, who appears often in these pages, was the American Ambassador in Rome. The friends and acquaintances who pass on Mussolini's remarks to her are high-placed officials. She learns of Russia's responses to the Italian government's moves from the Russian *chargé d'affaires*. She is shown a letter from the American President. She discusses the projected exhibition celebrating the Fascists' twenty years in power with the woman who is designing it. A conversation between two of Mussolini's most trusted advisers, Volpi and Balbo, is passed on to her by Volpi's daughter. The rumours Origo retails are not just the tittle-tattle of the drawing room or the *piazza*, they represent what was being said in innermost political and diplomatic circles.

Her private life plays no part in the diary. She has set out here to describe not her own domestic affairs but a nation's, albeit from a highly personal point of view. The closest thing to a private family event here is the arrival (or non-arrival) of La Foce's new tractor. Iris's first child, Gianni, died of meningitis in 1933 when he was seven years old. She mourned him in tight-lipped silence: it was only in her old age that she began to talk about him, and then, one friend recalls, she couldn't stop, recounting the story of his pathetically short life to anyone who would listen. After his death followed seven childless years and then, in the period covered by this diary, she became pregnant again. Readers may be startled to find her casually alluding to the birth of her daughter Benedetta in 1940 after no previous hint that all the hectic activity over the previous months has been undertaken while she was pregnant.

She is as reticent about her situation as a foreign national as she is about her motherhood. In the run-up to war, all over Europe, people who found themselves in the wrong place at the wrong time were being interned. Iris arranged for her mother and stepfather – both British and still living in Italy – to be given special passports and hurried out to Switzerland. But she says nothing of her own predicament. She writes of having made a short visit to Switzerland with Antonio in August 1939. Though she doesn't say so, they had been to Lucerne to hear a concert. The conductor should have been Bruno Walter (who was Jewish), but he had pulled out. His daughter had been shot dead the day before by her Nazi husband, who then also shot himself. Toscanini took Walter's place on the podium. Iris doesn't mention the two deaths. She writes about the "houses trimmed with wooden lace and the Sunday picnic-parties by the streams". She records that, returning over the Simplon pass, they saw an Italian driver attempting to cross the border and being turned back by a carabiniere who said, "No more Italians jaunting abroad now!" The sight must have chilled her, but she doesn't mention that in crossing back into Italy she is committing herself to sitting out the war in a country where she is a resident alien. There will be no further chance to get out.

*

The diary is a curious mixture of news – both fake and genuine – rumour, comment and observation. Origo was to write later that she had joined "the wide captive audience, all the world over, listening to confused, discordant voices coming out of a little box". The radio is at the centre of this diary. Iris and Antonio Origo and their friends gather round it, fiddle with the controls in an attempt to get the foreign stations, and anxiously discuss afterwards what they have heard. Mussolini knows how to exploit the medium. Propaganda pours over the airwaves. Discerning listeners like Iris sift the bombastic output for truth. "Far more than the whistle and crash of falling shells later on, or the dull roar of bomber formations over head," she wrote afterwards, "this cacophony represents my personal nightmare of the years before and during the war." Speeches from Hitler and Dolfuss, Eden and Chamberlain, the voices of schoolchildren or soldiers belting out Fascist anthems. "It is difficult to convey the cumulative impact of these voices, as we sat alone in the library of our isolated country house day after day, and the increasing sense they brought of inevitable, imminent catastrophe, of the Juggernaut approach of war." Difficult it may be, but in this remarkable diary, she conveys it – all the anxiety and uncertainty, all the bafflement and frustration of a clever, well-informed person striving to make sense of a crazy situation.

At La Foce the workers simply cannot believe war will come – even after it has actually been declared and their boys are being dragged off to fight. Iris almost shares their incredulity. How can Italy be sacrificing its young men on behalf of an ally who is so generally detested? (Italy fought against Austria and Germany in the First World War. The German-speaking peoples who had so long – as representatives of the Hapsburg Empire – dominated and oppressed Italians were described by d'Annunzio in the run-up to that first war as Italy's 'hereditary enemy'.) How can the supple shifts and rich ambiguities of intellectual discourse be replaced by crude propaganda? These questions are unanswerable. What Iris Origo captures here, poignantly and with great clarity, is the silence that falls when peace-time debate is replaced by the brute simplicity of armed combat.

*

One of this diary's most memorable entries is that describing June 10, 1940. A message comes from the local *fascio* ordering that all the estate's working men should gather to hear a broadcast at 5 p.m. The radio is carried out to the loggia and some hundred people are assembled. At five it is announced that the important speech is postponed for an hour. Bathos. The men sit on the ground, bring out bread and wine, play cards. "Antonio and the keepers discuss the young partridges and the twin calves born that morning: one of them will not live. I go indoors again; a great bowl of delphinium and lupins take me back for a moment to an English garden. A whiff of jasmine blows in at the window. It is all curiously unreal and also <u>boring</u>." The broadcast resumes. Mussolini announces, with much bombast, that Italy is declaring war on France and Britain. Afterwards, "The men shuffle away in silence. We go back into the house and stand looking at each other. 'Well, *ci siamo!*' says Antonio. 'I'm going out to look at the wheat.' Flatly, gloomily, we go to fetch our hats and coats."

At that moment, conscious of what is to come and their disparate views on it, they have nothing to say to each other, but Iris Origo, of whom Frances Partridge once said that she was so perceptive that in conversation with her "you felt bored into", could not be stunned into inarticulacy. In this unique and valuable diary, she conveys bewilderment and frustration, but she does so with such lucid intelligence and energy

---

* This is it!

that volumes of historians' generalisations drop away
to be replaced by knife-sharp detail. The black-shirted
squadristi, whose clothes strain over their pot-bellies,
and who apologise politely when they tread on her
toes in a crowded railway compartment. The air-raid
shelter rigged up in the colonnades of the Doge's
Palace. The governess, an elderly lady from Alsace-
Lorraine to whom Origo gives a lift, in floods of tears
at finding herself, for the second time in her life, an
enemy alien. The shaking of an old man's hand as he
takes Origo's arm to tell her that if the four sons who
work his farm are called up, he might as well drown
himself in the ditch at once. The bad faith of a press
which publishes articles about the deleterious effects of
coffee just as coffee becomes unobtainable, and which
greets meat-rationing with pieces extolling the bene-
fits of vegetarianism. The young soldier, awkward in
a stiff new uniform, crouching down to make a chain
of dandelions for his tiny daughter. William Phillips,
having lost his way, arriving late at a remote fishing
lodge to be greeted by "a very small, shabby man in a
brown overcoat who was standing waiting in the drizzle, quite alone" – the King of Italy. Vignettes like this
stud the pages of this diary, filling it with vivid flashes
of keenly observed life.

Iris Origo was still the honest-eyed seer Virginia Woolf thought her. "She's clean and picks her feet up": Woolf's gnomic comment is given substance by this diary. Origo's mind – clean of muzziness – bores into what she sees. Picking her feet up, refusing to be hobbled by prejudice or sentimentality, she gives a perceptive, poignant and often surprising account of a strange time.

Lucy Hughes-Hallett

1939

The train is packed; a thousand *squadristi* are on their way to Rome. The *squadristi* are the Fascists *della prima ora*, those who belonged to the first squads of 1919. They are going home to celebrate the 20th Anniversary of the foundation of the *Fasci* and to hear the Duce's speech tomorrow.

The six in our carriage are all middle-aged men – stoutish, with their black shirts bulging at the waist; their boots, too, have an air of being too tight for them. From their conversation we realize that they are business-men, and from the North: three Veneti, two Milanesi and a Romagnolo. One of them has a bicycle factory; one (the Romagnolo), is at the head of some co-operative stores. Now and again acquaintances in the corridor catch sight of them and come in to join them (apologizing politely for treading on my toes). The atmosphere is that of a college reunion – embraces, chaff, personal remarks; a hearty, a wholly masculine world. Is the heartiness a little forced? After a while there is silence; our companions take up their papers. The front page is wholly given up to themselves – "our glorious *squadristi*...". They put the papers down again. One of them – an elderly, grey-haired Venetian – shrugs his shoulders. "Well, we'll know something more tomorrow. I don't care what anyone else says. Tomorrow we'll know what *He* says – *il Capo!*" I look across at him – a quiet, sensible, placid family man; there is no mistaking the genuine fervour of his tone. Everyone in the carriage agrees: "It isn't only what he *says* – it's the whole construction behind it! In these twenty years – look where we've got to! I remember in 1919...." and the reminiscences begin again.

MARCH 28TH

Well, he has spoken. These same middle-aged *padri di famiglia* have shouted "No, no!" when asked whether they want "Honours? Rewards? Or an easier life?" They have accepted the axiom that "perpetual peace would be a catastrophe for human civilization" and the order to arm "at whatever cost, by whatever means, even if it should mean a *tabula rasa* of all that is meant by civilized life."

The applause, however, is definitely less intense than on previous occasions. It is a cold, wet day, and many of the *squadristi* have slept in tents at the Parioli; but there is also another chill in the air: the universal distaste for Germany as an ally. The part of the speech received with the least applause is that which reaffirms the solidity of the Axis, but afterwards the prevailing comment is: "What else could he say? It's England and France who have forced us into this position." There is considerable relief, however, at the loophole still left for negotiation with France.

Later in the day we walk about town. Everywhere the pavements are crowded with *squadristi*; they are walking up and down the *Corso* in parties of four or five, arm in arm. They are sitting at the cafés, they are flinging halfpennies (to ensure their return) into the Fontana di Trevi. They look – except for their shirts – good-natured, friendly and peace-loving. About 80% of them belong unmistakably to the working-class; the others look like small tradesmen or employees. Impossible not to like them; impossible too not to feel that Fascism was, in its beginnings, a genuine revolutionary movement of the people. Easy to see how they have been worked up to hatred of the countries presented to them as "obese, capitalistic, decadent" – to identify Fascism with the good of the working-class. Terrible to think of them fighting in Spain against men so like themselves. Terrible to think of what may lie ahead.

MARCH 30TH

The streets of Florence are hung with flags, to celebrate the fall of Madrid.

LA FOCE, MARCH 31ST

This year's new recruits have just been called up, those of 1912, and at every little station the platforms are crowded with groups of bewildered country boys with their bundles or little fibre suitcases – sitting on the edge of the platform, or standing about aimlessly, with the dazed, patient look of their own cattle.

Here, too, some of our peasants have gone (about

twenty-five so far). When we go round the farms their wives and mothers come hurrying out. "What do you say? There won't really be trouble, will there? It isn't really anything to do with us?" A few of the ones who went first have sent back postcards, saying that they are "on an island." Another says, "I can see nothing but rocks and sea and sky." (Pantelleria? Leros?)

Meanwhile there is a lull in the press propaganda. Daladier's speech – which might well have provoked a violent reaction (with its declaration: "Not an inch of our land, not a single one of our rights!") has been commented on with moderation. In Calabria Mussolini has said "Italy can afford to wait."

There is an immediate, disproportionate reaction towards optimism – and an even greater frankness of speech against Germany.

One young officer (recently back from Abyssinia) says that the army is intensely anti-German. The King anti-war. If there should be a division of opinion on the subject between the King and Mussolini, the army would follow the King.

Another young officer tells me the following story. A few days ago a German plane crashed near Padua, killing five men. The Colonel of the local regiment, on hearing the news, shrugged and exclaimed (before all his officers!) *"Cinque di meno!"**

I listened to Mussolini's Calabrian speech in the street, in Florence, where a loud-speaker was relaying it. Gradually a large crowd formed. I was struck by the guarded, colourless expression on most of the men's faces – and the undisguised anxiety in the women's. The prolonged applause caused a look of exasperation to cross most faces, as it prevented one from hearing the end of some of the sentences. When it became clear that nothing vital was to be said, everybody gave a sigh of relief and, without any comment, went about their business.

APRIL IST

Chamberlain's pronouncement about Poland has been received with unexpected moderation in the press and with some enthusiasm privately – as being likely to put a brake on Hitler.

A country neighbour (small farmer – a shrewd, sensible, elderly man) has just been to lunch, and has made no bones about expressing his disgust at recent events. He is particularly indignant at Mussolini's phrase

---

* Five less of them!

about peace being "a menace to civilization". "What about Sweden and Norway?" he says. "Aren't they more civilized than us? And happier? Are the working classes less well treated there?" (This is unexpected; he would not have said this five years ago.) He tells us that all his peasants, like ours, are terrified. One young woman, who is just expecting her first baby, prays daily that it will be a girl. "What's the use of having boys if they'll take them away from me and kill them?"

APRIL 4TH

Just back from Rome for the day. Full of rumours: Italy is about to invade Albania; England was going to occupy Corfu and only desisted on being told that it would mean certain war; Germany has got no less than thirty divisions in Libya. What does appear to be true is that some more Italian troops have gone to Spain and are encamped along the Pyrenees. Rhodes also is full of troops. Rumours flying about too as to the inadequacy of war material (both in quality and quantity) – and that Italy could not last a month, etc.

Meanwhile the station is full of recruits waiting for trains to the South, and our train is packed with

German tourists. Some University students (dressed in scarlet university hats, brilliant striped pyjama-jackets, and playing mouth-organs up and down the corridors) mock them mildly.

APRIL 5TH

The press is becoming more violent again. Yesterday's papers attack Chamberlain's "intervention policy to guarantee the privileges of the obese nations". Long articles are written to prove that Poland, a Catholic country, will never subscribe to any alliance which will cause her to be dependent on the support of Russia. Gayda has written a virulent article today about the Franco-Italian agreement of 1935 as an impossible basis for negotiation. Manacorda ridicules "democratic senility" in France and England. And all papers agree in emphasizing Germany's determination not to permit the "plan of encirclement" formed by the "Pharisaic policy of London".

Mussolini's comment (to Béraud) on his own "extreme" propagandists: *"Dans une maison bien réglée tout sert, même les ordures."**

---

* In a well-ordered household everything is useful, even garbage.

APRIL 6TH

Today much prominence is given in the papers to the meeting at Innsbruck of the Italian and German Chiefs of Staff. Comment on the British treaty with Poland is very acid.

It is now clear what form propaganda, in case of war, will take. The whole problem will be presented as an economic one. The "democratic countries", i.e., the "haves", will be presented as permanently blocking the way of the "have-nots" to economic expansion. Germany and Italy must fight or submit to suffocation. This point of view is presented in *The Times* of April 4th as "the last ditch of the Axis argument". Nevertheless, it is a view sincerely held by many educated Italians, who are profoundly convinced that nothing except violence will induce the democracies to concede a re-distribution of raw materials and of colonies. Fascists are thus enabled to see the impending war as a struggle between the poor man and the rich – a genuine revolutionary movement.

APRIL 8TH

And now Albania. The news, foreshadowed in the English and French papers and wireless, came here (to the general public) as a bombshell: announced on the radio (just before the three-hour Good Friday services) at 10 a.m. The bulletin took the now familiar form of stating that the invasion was a measure necessary to "safeguard the peace" of the country invaded and to quell the "armed bands" patrolling it; it was further stated that there was "no resistance worthy of mention" except an attempt at resistance by 'bands' at Durazzo, and that the population is "cordial". The manifestos dropped by planes told the Albanians that "any resistance would be immediately suppressed". "Do not listen to the members of your government who have impoverished you and now want to lead you to shed your blood in vain. The Italian troops have come to establish order, justice and peace". Here a party of "orthodox" (Fascist) Italians merely laughed at the pretext of "quelling the brigands" – ("How much do you supposed they were paid?") – but were equally sceptical about the subsequent accounts of the invasion from Paris and London, which told of violent

resistance from the Albanians and of the bombardment of Durazzo. The ultimate result of unceasing
propaganda has now been to cancel out the effect of
all news alike. One man said to me, "The radio has
made fools of us all". Late last night a further Italian
bulletin stated that the accounts given in anti-Fascist
countries of the Albanian operations "are so fantastic
that it is not worth while to deny them – as they follow
the same methods adopted during the Ethiopian war.
*It is now known and proved that the Fascist régime uses one
method only: always to tell the truth*".

APRIL IITH

An uneasy Easter Saturday and Sunday, spent chiefly
in trying to get foreign stations on the radio. Am particularly struck by two facts:

1) None of my friends (though devout Catholics)
expresses any distaste at the choice of Good Friday for
the invasion of Albania;

2) No-one (though all in private life honest and hon-
ourable men) shows the slightest interest in the terms
of either the Italo-Albanian Treaty of 1927, or of the
Anglo-Italian Agreement of last November.

On the other hand, their scepticism as to the facts supplied by their own papers or radio grows with every hour; and the disinclination for war. Also the certainty that war, if it does come, will be the end of Fascism.

Yesterday I went to Assisi for the day. The discontent there very great. Fresh men being called up every day. The complaints are quite open; Mussolini and Hitler referred to as *"quei due assassini".* One man, a blacksmith, says openly that if he is called up he will take the first opportunity to desert to the other side – and that all his friends feel the same. The *Pretore* – a noted anti-Fascist – belongs to the small number of people who will welcome a war, as bringing the certain downfall of Mussolini.

Today a friend arrives from Bologna. He says that there too discontent is widespread and violent. There are scenes in the streets of women clinging to men who are called up, as they leave. Bitter resentment is felt in all classes at being kept in the dark. I can find no traces of the violent anti-English or anti-French feeling so prevalent during the Abyssinian war; but anti-German feeling is rampant everywhere.

A young typist, married a year ago and with a small

---

* Those two murderers.

baby, writes today from Florence to tell me that her husband has been called up and sent to Albania. A pitiful letter. "I know that thousands of wives and mothers are in the same position as I, and I feel very selfish at only going on thinking about myself – but I can't help it... It isn't only now. I go on thinking that one day my Fabrizio (the baby), for whom my husband and I have made such a lot of plans, will be taken away from me, as my husband is now. What's the use of it all? What's the use of struggling on? We don't care how hard we work if only they'd leave us alone. But they won't."

One and a half million men have now been called up. The expense must be terrific. For that reason, apart from all others, it seems impossible that the crisis can be delayed long.

APRIL 13TH

Late last night an official announcement on the radio declared that "unless exceptional circumstances arise" no more recruits will be called up. This statement certainly aims at calming the widespread uneasiness and discontent – it seems to have been immediately successful.

The papers continue to have articles on the "encir-clement policy" of Britain. Gayda says that Britain has no right to take a moral line about Albania while she occupies Gibraltar, which belongs to Spain – Suez, which belongs to Egypt – Malta, which belongs to Italy, and Palestine, which belongs to the Arabs.

APRIL 14TH

A story from Rome. Two members of the Fascist party are talking in a café. A. talks scornfully about Ciano: his abominable manners, his callowness, his pro-German policy. B. defends him: "He's got the faults of youth, but he's able and he'll grow out of them". The next day B. is sent for and told to give up his Party membership card. "But I defended Ciano!" he protests. "That's not enough. You should have denounced your friend to the police."

MAY 12TH

There is now a curious lull. In spite of Poland, in spite of the German staff officers at the Review in Rome on the 9th, in spite of all the propaganda in the press against the "encirclement" policy of the democracies (now fully believed in by everyone), the general public has decided that there won't be a war, after all. The crowds listening to the radio bulletins in the squares and cafés are smaller; public works are in full swing; the theatres at the Florence *Maggio Musicale* are more crowded (though there are practically no foreigners) than I have ever seen them. That this temporary sense of security is deliberately fostered there can be no doubt (I heard it said of one man, who had been advising some English old ladies to go home, that he ought to be exiled as an alarmist). What lies behind it? Two things, I imagine. First, a wish to calm the agitation and discontent so prevalent last month, when war seemed imminent. But secondly – and more important – a determination to convince the general public that the real warmongers and alarmists are on the other side. The Fascist countries only want "peace and justice". Thus, if war does come, public opinion will be prepared to believe that it is the democracies who are responsible, and that the Fascist countries have been forced into it in self-defence.

MAY 13TH

A sinister remark of Mussolini's, said to an old friend (and official) in Romagna, who was asking him, a little anxiously, about the future: "*Stai tranquillo, erediteremo ancora*".* Inherit what? From whom? One can only inherit from the dead – in the sense that Austria and Czechoslovakia are now dead.

MAY 14TH

Mussolini's speech this morning in Turin comes as a confirmation of what I wrote two days ago, about attempting to put the responsibility for war on to the democracies. The speech – which was received with greater enthusiasm than other recent ones – is extremely clever. While leaving Italians with a clear impression that their leader doesn't want war, it prepares them – if war <u>does</u> come – to the belief that it is the democracies, in their "fury" against Germany and Italy, who have provoked it; meanwhile, they are to regard their own rearmament, which is to continue

---

* Don't worry, we'll inherit some more.

as hard as ever, as "a measure of self-protection, to safeguard the peace of Europe". All this has gone down very well, and the headlines of today's papers speak of "the grave responsibilities of the democracies". Moreover, Dean Inge obligingly chose yesterday to say that "it is not Germany and Italy, but England, who will be responsible for war", and to attack the "preponderant influence of the Jews on the press and the House of Commons". His remarks have been quoted in even the smallest provincial papers here.

And indeed, to the best of my belief, the truth is that Mussolini does not want war. He has never wanted a real war – only, at home, the "heroic" state of mind which its imminence produces (and which he achieved by such minor campaigns as Abyssinia and Spain) and abroad, the achievement of his expansionist aims. He does not want war now because he believes that he can achieve these aims without it. It remains to be seen whether he is right.

MAY 16TH

Yesterday Mussolini visited Cavour's grave, and stood some time in meditation beside it. It was Cavour who said: "If we did for ourselves what we do for our country, we should be the greatest of blackguards".

JUNE 26TH

The virulence of the recent press attacks on England and the open *Schadenfreude* over the events at Tientsin appear to be an echo of similar articles in Germany; the tone is that of nations already at war. It looks as if there would now be an unceasing blast of propaganda of this nature from now on until the autumn: as a preparation for war if necessary, otherwise as bluff. As propaganda, in these last two months, it seems to have failed in diminishing the average citizen's instinctive dislike of Germany, but it has succeeded:

1) in embedding the word and idea of "encirclement" in his mind;

2) in convincing him that, if there *is* a war, "the democracies" (to repeat what is now the stock phrase in everybody's mouth) "will be fighting for their privileges; Italy and Germany for their life."

JUNE 30TH

I have heard on the radio an interesting piece of propaganda: a Catholic broadcast in Germany (I think from the Vatican) on the occasion of St. Peter's Day. After an account of St. Peter's life, persecution and death on the Cross, the preacher proceeded to an exhortation to the persecuted Christians of our time. "The Church", he said, "has been hated and persecuted up to our own time... she will always be hated, because her thoughts are those of God and not of man. But the Church, through all persecutions, has always won. Peter died on the Cross, Peter is victorious." The exhortation which then followed might have been addressed to the Early Christians of St. Peter's own day. I wonder by whom it was heard in Germany, and under what conditions. The sermon ended with the words: "The Cross is our certain lot. *In Christ ist Sieg und Heil.*"

JULY 2ND

Lord Halifax's speech at Chatham House has loosed a fresh torrent of invective against England. I heard the original on the radio and could hardly recognize it in the version that I read the next morning in the papers here. Actually the greater part of what he said was quoted (not quite all) – but the emphasis was so presented that it produced an impression of unmitigated hypocrisy and duplicity. It is now the belief of most Fascists that it <u>may</u> be possible to extract from England a portion of what they want from her (re-division of colonies, re-distribution of raw materials, "freedom in the Mediterranean", etc.) but <u>only</u> by continued pressure and the constant menace (not reality) of war. They admit that this is a dangerous game (the more honest, even, that it is a revolting game) but say: "We've been forced into it. We have no other way of obtaining justice." This policy is based on the belief, on the one hand, that England won't fight if she can possibly help it (not for idealistic reasons, but because the more prosperous of two adversaries is always the one who has most to lose) and on the other, that she will not yield *anything* except under the threat of violence. "If we show even a single sign of yielding, or of being prepared to meet her halfway, we are done for."

This appears to be deadlock.

JULY 3RD

Much has been made in the press of the "dangerous alarmism" and "decadent panic" of the democracies (especially England) in this last week, and especially over the weekend; it is contrasted, of course, with the "grim serenity" here. The tone of the papers, however, is so angry that one wonders what underlies it. Meanwhile the accounts of events in the Far East and in Palestine and, above all, of the negotiations with Russia, continue to present English foreign policy as tortuous, hypocritical and totally ineffective.

JULY 4TH

To me one of the most alarming – as well as ugliest – symptoms of the moment is the growing tendency (on both sides) to deny any sincerity or good faith to their opponents. If there is a naïveté in too blind a faith in the essential decency of human nature, there is also a naïveté of a more dangerous kind in denying <u>any</u> idealistic motives to one's opponents. To do this is not only to make a psychological mistake; it is greatly to under-rate the strength of one's enemy.

JULY 5TH

Yesterday, driving through Scandicci (where there is a large home for permanently disabled soldiers) I met, in his wheelchair, one of the most terrible "grands mutilés" of the 1914–18 war that I have ever seen. Both legs gone, blind, and most horribly disfigured – and still alive, after twenty years.

And in 1959?

JULY 6TH

The latest caricature in *La Stampa* represents a singularly oafish and knock-kneed John Bull letting down his pants so that a small grinning Japanese soldier may prod his buttocks with a bayonet.

JULY 7TH

William Phillips (the US Ambassador and my godfather) who is here for the weekend, is determinedly optimistic in his certainty that war will be avoided this summer. He appears to base this conviction on the belief:

a) that Germany is not yet ready for war – not being yet satisfied with the progress of her "peaceful" penetration in the Balkans;

b) that Italy does not intend – if she can possibly avoid it – to fight at all.

He admits, however, that one of the chief dangerpoints is Hitler's belief (in spite of the speeches of Lord Halifax or anyone else) that England is now to be numbered among the "defeatist" peoples and that, to quote *Mein Kampf*, "in dealing with a people that has grown defeatist he (the victor-dictator) can then rely on the fact that no single one of these further acts of oppression will seem a sufficient reason to take up arms". If he applies this theory to Danzig there will be war.

On the other hand, William Phillips' opinion is that in view of the recent trouble in Danzig there will

now be a lull – which Italy will use quietly and unob-
trusively to occupy some of the "ancient Venetian"
cities of the Dalmatian coast – thus further strength-
ening her stranglehold on the Adriatic. Prince Paul of
Yugoslavia (whom W.P. visited recently) is fully aware
of this danger; and sees no means of defending those
cities. Certainly no one else will. It may have been this
move (among others) which Mussolini had in mind
with his phrase *"erediteremo ancora"*.

JULY 8TH

A curious – and perhaps significant – change in the
Italian press recently is the sympathetic tone now
adopted towards Russia (even including the quotation
of articles – anti-English ones of course – from the
Pravda). As the official press now takes its tone from
Germany, this suggests that there may be some foundation in the persistent rumours of a German-Russian
rapprochement. William Phillips says that, according to
the Russian *chargé d'affaires* in Rome (by far the ablest
and best informed of all his colleagues), *The Times* has
been quite unfailingly wrong over its account of the
negotiations in Moscow. The truth about the progress

of the negotiations (according to the news the Soviet diplomat received direct from Moscow) was generally the exact opposite of what *The Times* said; or, when the paper got the facts right, the interpretation was mistaken. Meanwhile there has been no reference whatever in Italy to the plans – already known in England and America – for the emigration of the population of the South Tyrol. That the 10,000 members of the population who are still German subjects should be transferred to the other side of the frontier is possibly desirable, but the choice offered to the rest of the German-speaking population (about 200,000) is a very grim one: either to move to Germany or to Southern Italy. As Catholics, and as ardent Austrian nationalists who bitterly resented the *Anschluss*, they cannot but dread coming under the Nazi régime (far more severe, as they have already learned, than the Fascist). But equally, a move to Southern Italy, among an alien population and in completely unfamiliar conditions, must be profoundly distasteful. And they have also the peasant's deep attachment to their own bit of land. The point that is still uncertain is how much pressure will be used to force them to move.

JULY 9TH

Have been talking to William Phillips about America. He maintains that Congress's rebuff to the President over the arms embargo appeared more serious than it really is – for if war should break out the country would be swung in the only way the US ever is swung: on a wave of emotion. He is convinced that in that case the embargo would immediately be withdrawn. He says that Roosevelt has already decided not to stand for the third time, but is only postponing his statement of this decision so as to keep some control over Congress; and he (W.P.) fears a violent isolationist reaction when this is known.

A recent personal letter of the President's to William Phillips emphasized the increased violence of American public opinion against Italy, as well as Germany.

JULY 10TH

The latest news of Schuschnigg is that he is going mad. The form of torture used has been to deprive him of any rest; loud-speakers in his room and the sudden flashing of lights day and night; a revolver left on his table, in the hope of driving him to suicide. This has failed, but now his mind is giving way.

A few months ago William Phillips presented to Mussolini, unofficially, a proposal of Roosevelt's for the settlement of the Jews. It was that if England were to give (as apparently she was then prepared to do) the greater part of Kenya for the formation of an independent Jewish State, Italy would also cede the portion of Southern Abyssinia adjoining with Kenya. The plan was to be financed by America, England and Jews all over the world; and the inducement offered to Italy was the influx of trade into Abyssinia that such a settlement would bring. But Mussolini refused to hear of it.

The following puzzle is being circulated throughout the country, entitled *Chi vincerà la guerra?**

MU<u>S</u>SOLINI	?
HI<u>T</u>LER	?
CH<u>A</u>MBERLAIN	?
DA<u>L</u>ADIER	?
CH<u>I</u>	
VI<u>N</u>CERÀ	?

---

* Who will win the war?

The answer being the third letter downwards – STALIN.

JULY 12TH

Today a very intelligent Roman woman – a landscape gardener, who is on the executive committee of the 1942 Exhibition – has spent the day here. The figures being spent on the exhibition are fantastic: the estimate for the whole is three *milliards* (of lire). This includes a considerable number of permanent buildings: a *Palazzo dell'Arte* – a great church with a dome nearly as large as St. Peter's – a model housing district – three artificial lakes (each four times as large as Piazza Venezia) – a great canal and so on.

The estimate for flowers and plants alone is four million lire. Where can it all be coming from? The only encouraging aspect of it all is that surely even the present régime would not have the folly to spend so much on this work (which is proceeding steadily) if they seriously intended war.

The same woman – herself very anti-Fascist (and with Jewish connections) reports the usual discontent with the German alliance and with the increasing restrictions in every field, material and intellectual. But when I asked her whether any of her younger colleagues (those who have just left the University) would agree with her, she said, no. They have swallowed the Fascist theory whole. I was, however, interested to see how very well informed she and her friends manage to be – even about foreign news. Her brother-in-law has added a transmitting apparatus (made by himself) to his radio, and is in continual communication with friends in England.

A little boy of ten, the son of one of my friends, was highly praised for his school essay, which was full of the most orthodox Fascist sentiments. When he brought home a rough copy, his mother asked him: "Do you really believe all this, Luigino?" "Oh no, mother, of course not! But it is the only way to get good marks."

JULY 13TH

The news of the expulsion – at forty-eight hours' notice – of all foreigners from the province of Bolzano came as a thunderbolt here – although already announced in the English papers and by the BBC on the evening of the 11th. Today articles in the papers attempt to minimize its importance, describing it as a "police measure" rendered necessary by discoveries of the OVRA* of "the activities of certain members of Western nations" in the district. Still no reference whatever is made to the plan of evacuation of the Tyrolese population.

Fascists, who are extremely resentful of any suggestion that Italy is becoming a "vassal state" of Germany, point triumphantly to this measure – and to the forts that are being built on the Brenner – as a proof that Italian policy still maintains its independence. Surely, however, it is a proof of exactly the contrary: a sop to Germany for disregarding this "minority" alone.

JULY 15TH

Yesterday, in the train, an unpleasant conversation with S., the head of a small private bank in Rome – a man who goes about a good deal in the "smart" cosmopolitan set, and who was just back from England. Starting by deploring the expulsion of foreigners from the Tyrol, he began – very cautiously at

---

* Secret police.

first – to attack the Fascist régime: lack of freedom, grim prospects ahead financially, general discontent, comparisons with England, etc. etc. I agreed with his sentiments and yet felt uncomfortable – there was something wrong. Then, as he went on, I realized that everything he was deploring in the present world was the good side: the revolutionary, vital, idealistic element. Everything he wished to preserve (and admired in England, for instance) was based on the rule of money – and the power which money brings. Peace and war, the Jewish question, the social question, the situation in China, every subject under the sun, was seen only in its relation to vested interests. So complete, so whole-hearted was his preoccupation that after an hour's conversation I began to wonder whether I had not been incredibly naïve in believing there was any other governing motive in human life. I thought of people like Max, Olaf, Macmurray* and felt the forces up against them to be terrifyingly, overwhelmingly strong. They seem to belong to a whole different planet.

And yet – to undervalue the power of idealism (even mistaken idealism?) is surely also a mistake. Sometimes it is the apparently naïve who are the realists.

---

* Max Plowman, Olaf Bryn Kullmann, John Macmurray.

VENICE, JULY 16TH

It is curious – the unanimity with which everyone here refuses to believe in the possibility of war. I don't mean only the general public, who don't know the facts, but also people who do. Everyone I have seen in the last few days (S., the banker; Volpi's daughter, who had just been talking to Balbo; General R., William Phillips, representing the diplomatic opinion in Rome) all agree that there won't (some say "can't") be war. I do not get the impression this is merely wishful thinking. I expect that they are entirely right in saying that Mussolini intends to avoid war – knows, indeed, that though he might swing his country into it, there would be a revolution within a few months. But this may be a miscalculation:

1) of Mussolini's capacity to act as a moderating influence on Hitler;

2) of the amount which (as Fascists believe) can be obtained from the democracies by the present system of unceasing tension.

Venice is empty of tourists. Even Germans have stopped coming – because of the large German debt to Italy. (Even payments to the Italian workmen in

Germany take six or seven months to reach their families, being paid not in cash but through "clearing"). *"Eh, signora, la politica!"* says the gondolier in a tone of disgust. "Well, so long as there's no war!" says the hairdresser. "Better tighten your belt a bit than be killed."

Today I have seen here – under the arcade of the Doges' Palaces – the first and only air-raid shelter for the general public that I have yet seen in Italy.

ROME, JULY 17TH

William Phillips tells me that his naval and air attachés, both just back from a tour in the North, saw no traces of preparations for immediate war anywhere – not even in the great steel factories. Of course, it is <u>possible</u> that Mussolini, after all, intends to keep out even if Germany comes in, but it does not now seem to me <u>likely</u>. Perhaps not even possible.

Meanwhile there seems to be a complete muddle going on in the Tyrol. Several people (including two American families) who produced a doctor's certificate have been allowed to stay on. Bastianini, whom Phillips went to see about it at the F.O. (in Ciano's absence) said that the order (of expelling foreigners) came as a complete surprise to him too – and that he has no idea what it's all about. It is all very odd. It does not hang together. For instance, the British Minister to the Vatican, D'Arcy Osborne, who had engaged rooms at Carezza (Karersee) for the summer, wrote after the decree cancelling them. He immediately received a letter from the hotel manager begging him to come all the same and enclosing a special permit from the Prefect of the province! This does not fit in with the theory that they want to get rid of all foreign observers (D.O. is not known as pro-Fascist).

JULY 18TH

Had a long talk after dinner with a young University law student – an intelligent, enthusiastic, sensitive, imprudent young man – who is just about to prepare his *tesi di laurea* – and whose greatest ambition is one day to be a member of the International Court at the Hague. He went to his professor, as is the custom, to discuss what theme he should choose. "I think," he said, "I should like to discuss – from a purely judicial

point of view, of course – the question of the difference between rights and aspirations." "Oh!" said the
professor, "Well – I think perhaps I shouldn't raise
that point just now." "Well, then, I had thought of
non-intervention as a possible subject?" "Well, perhaps
not that either." "Or the judicial position of the participants in non-declared wars?" "No, no, certainly not."
"Or the clause *rebus sic stantibus* in relation to Article
10 of the Covenant?" "Good God, no!" The theme is
not yet chosen.

A very little questioning was enough to produce
the information that the young man belongs to a
small but ardent group of university students, determined to find out what is being thought, felt and
taught in other countries. He told me how he had
smuggled in one of Croce's articles (on dictatorship –
published in *The New Republic*) and of how he and his
friends sat up at night copying it, to hand on to other
people.

We talked about the Risorgimento leaders: Mazzini,
Cavour. "Yes," he said, "but they were so busy freeing
Italians from the Austrians that they never had time
to conceive that real freedom is a quality in oneself!" I
quoted Cavour's "We have created Italy; now we must
create Italians." "Yes," he said bitterly, "and since then

they've 'created' an Empire, and still there aren't any Italians!"

He told me, too, of a group of communist students at the University, with whom the young liberals, while not wholly sharing their views, are in touch – sharing with them a common indignation and a common thirst for news. But the communists are very careful. They do not even, he told me (not without a certain babyish 'secret-society' pride), know each other's names. Each one only knows one other member, to whom he passes on news and orders, and he in turn hands them on to one other. Meanwhile, they and the liberals agree in believing that war – if it does come – will give them their chance. "To those of us who survive," the boy added grimly, looking quite absurdly young. I wish I could convey his odd mixture of childish pride at belonging to "the minority", of real intelligence, and of something very sincere and tragic. It's the tragic impression that has remained with me.

There is a general tightening up of rules (presumably due to the Germans) about any form of importation – from news and books to material objects. A friend in the North, who used to receive foreign papers, writes that *Le Temps*, *Le Figaro* and *Le*

Jour are now all held up; the only one which he still gets is the *Journal de Genève*. Recently we had obtained (with great difficulty, and only by proving that it would be paid for with money already abroad) an importation permit for an American tractor. The permit was already in our hands when suddenly, a few days ago, a telegram came saying that the permit was revoked and must be returned immediately. Antonio went next day to the Ministry of Agriculture, and was told that this measure was a "reprisal" for "outrageous" duties recently placed on Italian silks in America, and that seventy other permits for tractors were stopped at the same time as ours. William Phillips, who has been going into the matter, says that the duty in question is, on the contrary, a very small one, and limited only to a small number of printed silks of exclusively Italian design. This (what I told him about the tractors) is the first he has heard of "reprisals". And so it goes on.

JULY 19TH

This morning an American journalist, just back from a tour in the Tyrol, brought back the following report to the American Ambassador.

1) <u>German subjects</u> are to move to Germany, but will be allowed three months in which to do so.

2) <u>Italian subjects of Austrian origin</u> are to move either to Germany or to other Italian provinces, but are nominally to be allowed two years in which to do so, in the case of owners of property, and one year in the case of non-landowners. In actual practice, however, those who own no property will have to go much sooner, as all employers, hotel-keepers, etc., are being instructed to refuse employment to such persons, who will at the same time be told that good work and good pay are waiting for them on the same side of the frontier. Presumably this is the aspect to which Sig. Gayda refers when he says that the "voluntary exodus... will be assisted by the two Governments both at the point of departure and of arrival!"

LA FOCE, JULY 20TH

Have just been to tea with some charming anti-Fascist neighbours, the Braccis. They – and, they say, all their friends – are very pessimistic about the prospects of war and regard the optimism of Fascist circles as either propaganda or wishful thinking. Contessa Bracci, who has two sons of twenty-two and nineteen, is particularly depressed. "It would be bad enough," she says, "if they were going to fight for something that they believe in. But to know that they will be fighting for what they hate and despise…" There was much discussion as to whether Italy, at the last moment, could and would wriggle out, but the rumour now current is that Hitler will take steps to prevent this by starting the conflagration in Tunis (with the manufactured murder of some Italians there) and only afterwards seizing Danzig.

JULY 21ST

The measures for the agricultural development of Sicily, announced yesterday, have my greatest sympathy. I only hope they will be extended later (as is doubtless intended) to Calabria and other regions of the South, where enormous tracts of property are held by absentee landlords. The apathy and cupidity of these landowners and the consequent misery of the peasants has been a disgrace for centuries. Enormous tracts of potentially fertile land lie fallow or are given up to pasture; moreover, being let out to middlemen, who in their turn rent the land to other smaller middlemen, the shepherd or peasant who is at the bottom of the long ladder leads a life that is close to starvation. In Calabria, a few years ago, whole families were living in wretched reed huts. On inquiring whether these were temporary habitations used only during harvest-time, the reply was that they were lived in all the year round; the peasants were <u>forbidden</u> by the landowners to put up any more permanent building, since this would give them, after a certain number of years, squatters' rights – i.e. a claim to the land on which they had built; and this was against the interests both of landowners and middlemen. The great plain of Sybaris, renowned in classical days for its fabulous riches, was in this condition but has since been taken over by the government and put under cultivation. Now the same is to be done for Sicily. The scheme comprises the building of 20,000 farms and an extensive system of road-building and irrigation. The social reform implied is one of great importance, since it is stated that if the landowners refuse or declare themselves unable to undertake the work (for which, in addition to the part carried out exclusively by the State, special loans will be granted) their land will be confiscated. When the landowners are prepared to collaborate in the new work the whole or part of the land will 'eventually' be returned to them; when they refuse to collaborate they will be expropriated. This is the first application on a large scale of the expropriation of property, which has already been applied in a few cases in other agricultural districts.

It is also significant of a return to the Duce's policy of a few years ago – of developing the resources of his own country first – and may perhaps be taken as an indication of the difficulties and disappointments encountered in Abyssinia.

Finally, this particular decision has been taken here as a sign of the Duce's wish for peace; of his intention to turn back the country's energies towards constructive and not destructive work. It is, in any case, a highly intelligent step and may possibly be indicative of a wider change of policy.

It is also possible (reading between the lines of the press comments on this measure, asking: "What countries clearly show that they mean peace, not war? Which are those that genuinely seek the interests of the people?") that there may be an intention of creating a favourable effect in Russia; for undoubtedly both Italy and Germany are doing all they can to start negotiations of their own with the USSR. But whatever the motive, and however imperfect the execution, the measure is a good one – for the simple reason that each of these measures, in social terms, represents something from which there is no going back. The Southern peasant, once he has lived in a decent house, cultivated his land rationally, and sent his children to school – will not, under <u>any</u> political régime, go back to his house of reeds. The steps which produce a development of human awareness are irrevocable; no adult can become a child again.

JULY 30TH

I am now staying with the Sennis – an old-fashioned "black" Roman family*. An American mother and four grown-up sons, two of whom fought in Abyssinia (one still in the regular army, the other in the Breda works in Milan). Their grandfather belonged to the *guardia nobile†* and their uncle, who is also here, in the diplomatic service, has been for five years Mussolini's *capo del cerimoniale*. The Sennis are all Fascists, but they are Catholics first; where there is a clash between the two Catholicism wins. Moreover they pride themselves on not being cut off from news from abroad. They

---

* The Black Nobility are the Roman families who remained loyal to the Pope after 1870, when Rome became part of the Kingdom of Italy under the Savoy family.
† The Pope's aristocratic guard.

read assiduously not only the Italian papers and the *Osservatore Romano*, but *The Times*, *Le Temps* and the *Journal de Genève*; they listen every day to the news from the BBC and Paris PTT. They are intensely anti-German, mildly anti-French and inclined, even now, to like England (Chamberlain's England). Two of them went to Oxford; all have many English friends. They deplore the "necessity" of the Axis, feel a mild aversion to anti-Semitism and wholeheartedly deplore and condemn (on moral and religious grounds) the Anglo-Franco approach to Russia. Their Catholicism and their aristocratic traditions combine and blind them to the fundamental ungenerosity of their attitude; but they would be profoundly shocked if this was suggested to them. Affectionate and high-principled in their private lives, they one and all totally drop these principles and sentiments as soon as any political issue is discussed – and the word "realistic" is seldom off their lips.

The son, now employed at the Breda arms factory, described with some humour how the Chinese and Japanese delegations, both seeking armament contracts, happened to arrive in Milan on the same day. The Japanese were received downstairs, in the *sala d'onore*, with a banquet and speeches; the Chinese were hustled up to a little bare office upstairs. "We did business with both, of course," he concluded.

JULY 31ST

Count Carlo Senni has just been talking about his years with Mussolini, to whom he is whole-heartedly, but not wholly uncritically, loyal. He emphasizes one trait which strikes everyone who has ever worked with Mussolini: his unbounded, almost undisguised, utterly cynical contempt for his own human instruments. Except for his brother Arnaldo (now dead) and perhaps, to a lesser extent, his daughter, there is no human being in the world whom he loves and trusts. He believes in the ability of his son-in-law; he does not trust him. A sentimentalist about "the people" en masse, he is completely cynical about all individuals, and measures them only by the use he can put them to... Yet so great is his personal ascendancy that his underlings – knowing that they themselves will be kicked away as soon as they cease to be useful – still retain their personal devotion to him.

According to Carlo Senni, one of the few people Mussolini really likes and respects is the King – and these

feelings are warmly reciprocated. It's impossible, he says, to
see the two men together without feeling how much they
like each other. (And this in spite of the fact that the King
is said to dislike the German alliance and to have used all
his influence, at every point, to avert war.) Moreover, in
the last two years the Prince of Piemonte is said to have
become on much better terms with Mussolini.

AUGUST 5TH

I have just been reading an article on anti-Semitism.
The writer of the article woke up every morning to
hear the news vendors cry: *"Achetez la Lutte – la lutte
anti-juive – le réveil anti-juif – l'anti-juif!"* On buying the
papers, he discovered that the editors made no secret
of their intentions: "We shall pass over the evil actions
committed by Christians and with the greatest care
reveal those committed by Jews." The papers also
contained – after the usual historical attack on the
Jews, corruptors of humanity – a list of Jewish usurers,
thieves, forgers, traitors, all mentioned by name; an
attack on all those who refuse to boycott Jewish goods
and shops, or dare to defend them; a touching incident
of "patriotic" children of five and six who tore another

little girl's pinafore to pieces and proudly exclaimed *"C'est une sale juive'"**; and finally an advertisement: *"Perinaud, Coiffeur, Prévient sa nombreuse Clientèle que dans son Magasin on ne rase pas les Juifs ni les Teigneux."*† The writer then proceeds to describe the burning of a synagogue, the destruction of the sacred books and the murder of a Jew by the crowd. He comments: "Anti-Semitism is the meeting-point of all that is most corrupt in a fanatical clergy, all that is most reactionary in the survivors of a feudal aristocracy and all that is most brutal in a revolutionary proletariat."

Hear, hear. What is curious is that this article was written in 1909 by Count Papafava, a progressive Italian Liberal, à propos of the Jewish persecution in Algeria!

AUGUST 6TH

Have again been to the Braccis and met there old Senator Albertini, for many years the editor of the *Corriere della Sera*. He seemed a quiet, honest-faced, nice, able man. He brought with him a page of *The Times* with Lord Halifax's last speech, which he then

---

* She's a dirty Jew.

† Perinaud, Hairdresser, warns his numerous clients that neither Jews nor Unpleasant Characters may be shaved in his shop.

translated for the others. Chamberlain was spoken of with dislike and mistrust, but Lord Halifax still with some confidence and hope. The truth is that, according to the company in which one happens to be, one knows beforehand what the opinion will be on any of the current topics. Among the anti-Fascists, Chamberlain is spoken of with contempt and Bonnet with loathing; Roosevelt is admired. In Fascist circles the odium falls on Churchill and on the Labour Party; Catholics unite to deplore the advances to Russia. Moreover one also knows beforehand where the blind spots will be. The Fascist averts his mind from the refugee problem and the situation in Czecho Slovakia ("All very much exaggerated – one must allow for foreign propaganda.") The Catholics turn a deaf ear to all accounts of executions in Spain; the anti-Fascist has seldom heard of any trouble in Russia. Only on one point are they all agreed: they don't want war.

A story is now current that one of the reasons for the extreme optimism of people in high Fascist circles is that the Italo-German military treaty was accompanied by a "secret letter" from Mussolini to Hitler definitely stating that under no circumstances would Italy be ready to take part in any war for another five years. I wonder.

AUGUST 27TH

It was strange, crossing the frontier. All the afternoon we had driven up the neat, green little Swiss valleys, past the houses trimmed with wooden lace and the Sunday picnic-parties by the streams. At Martigny we lunched on trout and listened to the news; then we began to climb the pass. There were two or three Italian cars going in the same direction as ourselves and a few French and English ones going the other way; but not the most fertile imagination could find any traces of war upon the Simplon. One single defile of the pass, on the Swiss side, was fortified, manned by a few moon-faced soldiers, and on the other side a squad of twenty *alpini* were singing to a concertina. But as we stood waiting for the Customs examination, an Italian car which had driven up a few minutes before, bound for Switzerland, backed, turned, and drove back to Italy again. "No more Italians jaunting abroad now, and none of our money!" said the *carabiniere* with a friendly grin, as he handed back our passports. "Come in, and stay in!" The pole of the barrier swung slowly back behind us.

But on the way to Milan, no trace of tension or

war-fever was to be seen. It was a fine Sunday evening and all along the lake, parties of young people were dancing and singing. Even at Milan station, no troops. The papers, too, were curiously moderate in tone. All the propaganda against England and France has ceased; *The Times* and *Le Temps* were on sale – indeed at most bookstalls were sold out as soon as they arrived. Why then did no one seem anxious? Why were there no war preparations? It all seemed very odd.

AUGUST 28TH

After a day in Florence, it is still puzzling. It is true that among educated people there is a good deal of anxiety; everyone listens four or five times a day to the radio and eagerly buys the foreign papers; most reserve officers have been called up and now six classes of recruits (about one and a half million men) and the navy and air force are fully mobilised. But in the *popolino* – so terrified last September and even at Easter – there is a curious calm. "Don't you worry, nothing's going to happen!" says the hairdresser, as he sees me reading the papers. "You'll see, the Duce will stop the war at the last moment," says the taxi-driver.

At the performance of *La Traviata* in Piazza della Signoria the moonlit square is packed with a gay, apparently carefree crowd. At the end of the second act, indeed, when the *Inno a Roma* was played in the interval before the broadcasting of the news, a sudden look of anxiety crossed the face of the audience; but as soon as it became evident that there was nothing new, they gave themselves up again to the sonorous melodies of the opera. "Look what Fascism has done for our people!" says a young officer as we walk home. "Compare their calm with the feverish tension in France and England!" But it isn't exactly calm. It is a mixture of passive fatalism, and of a genuine faith in their leader: the fruits of fifteen years of being taught not to think. It is certainly not a readiness for war, but merely a blind belief that, "somehow", it won't happen.

As we leave the house of some Italian friends in the country, we are asked to give a lift to their old governess, M.lle Marcaud, who appears in floods of tears. On the way down she tells us her story. A native of Alsace-Lorraine, she was a German in the last war, and is now a Frenchwoman, so that twice in the course of her obscure and blameless life she has been "an enemy alien" – on different sides! But in 1915, she cries, they let her stay in Italy, and now they have told her that she must go. She has no family to turn to, her home was destroyed in the last war, her few savings are in Italy, and she may take only 350 lire with her. We drop her, still in tears, at the French Consulate. How many thousand people will find themselves in positions like these in a few weeks' time?

AUGUST 29TH

Today the atmosphere is changing. Local regulations are bringing about a realisation of the situation, where the papers failed to do so. Yet the restrictions are, as yet, comparatively mild: all private motor-cars are to be stopped next Sunday, and restaurants are to be restricted to a single dish of either meat or fish. But now the town is full of wild rumours. An Italian division has been sent from Bologna to Nuremburg. The explanation of the Duce's silence is that he has had a stroke. The mysterious passenger on the plane that landed in England was Mussolini himself – no, Beck – no, Grandi. There is not even the faintest pretence of martial ardour.

In the evening we went to say goodbye to Nesta de Robeck, who is among the last English women to leave, except for a few very old ladies, who can't move. She has left me their names and addresses, in case they need help later on.

Here is a letter written yesterday by a young Italian to his mother. The writer, who is working in the Breda at Milan, took part in the Abyssinian war. "Will this war come? I can't believe it. Above all I can't believe that we shall be called upon to fight against people towards whom we have not got the slightest grudge and by the side of people we all despise. I have yet to find a single man who wants to fight on the side of the Germans! What is certain is that, politically speaking, we are passing from one absurdity to another. No one knows what to think: whether to wish that war come and be done with once and for all, or whether the problem of Danzig can be resolved by a complicated formula... But that would leave all the fundamental European problems still unresolved, and next year we should be *da capo*. And then (this is what really troubles me) with this falsification of our position, shall we be able to do our best? For we all feel this falsification, this forced alliance with Germany... Feeling neither any animosity towards our probable enemies, nor solidarity with our allies, people don't know how to behave. They argue, joke, laugh at the sensational headlines in the papers. But they don't really believe in the possibility of war. As you see, it is a nonchalant and cold vigil."

Nevertheless at the end of his letter he adds: "If war does come, I shall write at once to Gen. V. and ask to be transferred to my regiment. I don't want to miss the first few months, which are always the most exciting."

AUGUST 30TH

Still no more news, and we drove back to the country yesterday evening. A still, lovely summer's evening; the grapes ripening, the oxen ploughing. Only man is mad.

On our farm two of the *sotto-fattori* have been called up, and a good many of the peasants. They are very upset, but still do not realise that it is anything worse than Abyssinia or Spain. "We've had enough of this," is their refrain, *"ora basta.* We want to be left alone." But still dimly, blindly, they believe: "It won't come to a real war: the Duce will get us out of it somehow."

The sale of coffee is now forbidden and tea is unprocurable. All private cars are to be stopped on September 3rd.

We went to call on our old friends, the Bracci family, at Montepulciano, and found them very depressed. Always anti-Fascist, they see in the present events the fulfilment of their gloomiest prophecies. Their interpretation of Mussolini's complete silence and the general state of bewilderment, is that the German-Russian pact <u>was</u> made without Italy's knowledge, and that at this third concealment Mussolini's patience gave way. He is now merely engaged in attempting to get out of the alliance at some profit to himself. Yet another, that General Badoglio is imprisoned in his own house, for having refused to take command of the army. Some of these stories, if not all, must clearly be untrue!

I speak of the danger of another Munich, but they cut me short. "No, we can't believe that of England now! That isn't possible, whatever else may be." I say something about the curious fatalistic calm of the Florentine people. They say: "Not here! Here everyone is frankly terrified." And a friend from Piemonte adds: "And in Piemonte, angry. The men say quite openly: 'All right, give us arms, and you'll see what will happen!'". Someone adds, "That means revolution. And think of the horrors of the repressions at first!" – "It's the end of dictatorships, anyway." – "Yes, whether it's peace or war," everyone agrees. But there is too much sadness and anxiety to leave room for satisfaction.

AUGUST 31ST

Today the general mobilisation in Poland. The papers definitely more pro-German again. They quote at length the German denial that the Polish mobilisation was caused by the movement of German troops in Slovakia, and define it as "a fresh act of provocation". They attempt, too, to present Hitler's messages as a "noble gesture towards peace", and to throw the whole onus of responsibility upon England.

The kindergarten teacher, just arrived from Rome, reports that the people there are very puzzled and bewildered. "Why doesn't the Duce say something?" she exclaims. "He talked such a lot last September! We all went and shouted under his windows yesterday. At last he appeared – and said nothing at all. We all believe he could save us. Why doesn't he do it?"

The purchase of gas-masks has today been rendered obligatory for the personnel of hospitals, factories, charitable institutions, etc., but only for one fifth of the employees, and is "recommended" to private persons. Old people, women and children who have country homes are also advised to leave the larger cities, but there is no mention of any evacuation plans on a larger scale.

This afternoon we have been going round the farms. Everywhere the peasants come hurrying out to meet us, with the same anxious question: "What do <u>you</u> say? Will there be war?" From every farm at least one man has already been called up: "My Cecco went yesterday; my Beppe had his card this morning. What's going to happen to us?" One old man, whose four sons work on the farm, put a shaking hand on my arm and looked up into my face: "Please say something to cheer me up! If they all four go, I might as well throw myself into that ditch. Who will work the farm? What shall we give the children to eat?" What can one answer, except, "There is still hope."

SEPTEMBER IST

Yesterday evening late the news came: first, from Germany, the full text of the terms offered to Poland, and then the statement that, as these offers had not been followed by the arrival of a Polish representative, but by the mobilisation of Poland, Germany was obliged to consider her offer rejected. A quarter of an hour later the translation of the same communication came from England, followed by the statement that, until Poland's answer was known, it was not possible for England or France to offer any comment. Then came instructions for the evacuation of children from London and orders from the Admiralty and War Office.

At 1 p.m. today the news was even more bewildering. The Italian radio gave the full text of Hitler's speech to the Reichstag. Germany has proclaimed the union of Danzig with the Reich; German troops have invaded Poland as a measure of "active defence" (a new expression). Italy is given Germany's thanks for her "comprehension", but no word is said about her as an ally. Germany, Hitler says, will settle her problems alone. It seems clear that Hitler still hopes to limit the conflict. Total silence from Rome.

At 2 p.m. we are told that there will be a meeting in Rome this afternoon of the Grand Council, and in London of the House of Commons. The day's papers attempt to throw the whole blame for the catastrophe on the obstinacy of Poland and her "mad gesture" of mobilisation. The Führer, it is said, had by his "reason-able and logical proposals" done all that he could do to save the peace of Europe. The true responsibility lies with the great democracies, who are deliberately using Danzig as a pretext in the struggle for their own dwin-dling hegemony. The struggle is one between two conflicting interests: those of the nations who wish to preserve the "monstrous injustices" of Versailles, and those who wish for their revision as a basis for a permanent peace.

All afternoon I try in vain to get any French or English wireless station, for more accurate news. At 4.30, from Rome, comes the communiqué of the Roman Council: Mussolini approves the military measures already taken, which are of a purely pre-cautionary nature, and states that "Italy will take no military initiative." Then comes the telegram from Hitler, stating definitely that he does not require Italy's military assistance. What lies behind it all?

Finally, at 9 p.m., I hear from the BBC the full report of Chamberlain's speech and the denial that Germany's proposals were ever sent to Poland; she had no chance either to accept or refuse them, before the German army invaded her. To hear these clear, calm, and wholly convincing statements, after twenty-four hours of attacks on "the inexplicable reception given by the democracies to Germany's equitable terms", was a relief that cannot be described. Tragic as the news may be, and inevitable as the intervention of England and France now seems, the issue is at last a clear one.

SEPTEMBER 2ND

Today the Italian papers are strange reading. The interpretation of the news is indeed strongly pro-German. One headline reads: "The German army serves the cause of right and justice", and the leading article speaks of deliberate Polish aggression, and of the Polish "bellicose exaltation, aggressiveness, and forgetfulness of reality and of other people's rights." But in spite of this Chamberlain's speech is quoted in an accurate summary, giving especial prominence to his tribute to Mussolini's efforts for peace, and news from France is also given with fullness and moderation. Moreover last night there was no attempt to interrupt the foreign radio transmissions. Is one to conclude that Italy has definitely decided to be neutral? Those Fascists who now believe this to be likely, justify it by the part that Mussolini is to play as mediator, obtaining in that role the "revindication of the just rights" of Italy as well as Germany, as a stable basis for peace. "You'll see, they prophesy, it isn't too late even now! The Duce has never failed us yet; never has he failed to have a far-seeing, constructive policy. Now his time has come!" Their words do not sound like statements of opinion, but like affirmations of a creed.

This afternoon I went to see the Braccis, and with them listened to the French news – Daladier's speech to the Chamber, followed by the *Marseillaise*. My hosts spoke with great emotion and admiration of Chamberlain's speech. "Now there can't be a second Munich; England will fight for civilization – at last." Their interpretation was simple: Hitler has betrayed everyone in turn, and now Mussolini has betrayed him! He'll shilly-shally for a bit, and then strike a bargain with the highest bidder.

At 9 p.m. the startling declaration that the delay in the German news was "possibly due to a proposal" that a five-power conference should meet immediately, and adding the British stipulation that German troops must first retire from Poland. Went to bed not daring to hope again – and yet unable not to. Tomorrow at midday we shall know.

SEPTEMBER 3RD

We know – and it is war.

This morning – the last day that cars can be used – being a clear, cloudless day, we drove up into the hills to visit our old friends, the Senni family in Badia Prataglia, but as we drove along the Val di Chiana we saw in every village little groups of *richiamati** and women crying. We had meant to reach the Sennis in time for Chamberlain's statement, but as we drove up to the door, one of the boys came down to meet us: "The speech is just over. It's war."

I went quickly upstairs and found Mary Senni (American by birth) and Diana Bordonaro (half-English) by the radio, with tears in their eyes. Half an hour later Chamberlain's statement was repeated. When it was over, Mary came across to me: "If Italy comes in now on the German side, I shan't be able to bear it! I would have let my boys go, to fight for something they believed in; but now – not against civilization!"

All afternoon we sat round the radio, listening to one country after the other – Europe moving to war. Then the King's speech – slow and halting, but

---

* Reserve soldiers who have been called up.

somehow very moving – and "God save the King."

Later on we talk of the effect of all this on the Italian people. "Nothing", says Diana, "no propaganda, will ever persuade the Italian peasant and workman, that it was Chamberlain who wanted war. They'll know it was Hitler's fault." "Yes," says the son of twenty, "and the more time elapses, the more difficult it will be to persuade us to fight on the German side." But I am not quite so sure.

SEPTEMBER 5TH

Today Mussolini's statement is published, laying the onus of the declaration of war on Hitler, and presenting himself as the "single just man" who "made a last attempt to save the peace of Europe". According to his account, his proposal for a conference of the Five Powers was sent on August 31st to France and England, whose favourable reply only reached him on September 1st. But during the night "frontier incidents had occurred which determined the Führer to begin military operations against Poland." The French and English answers having been favourable (especially the French), Mussolini conveyed them to

Hitler, who replied that he would consider them, but not if they had the character of an ultimatum, and asked for twenty-four hours for consideration. Both his conditions were agreed to, but France and England insisted on the evacuation of Poland, previous to any conference.

The news of the sinking of the *Athenia* has been given in such a manner that people say, "God knows who really did it! It's certainly a very convenient piece of propaganda."

Today Antonio has been called up as an officer in the reserve. His regiment, which was in Albania, is to be re-formed in Florence, and he is to go there tomorrow.

SEPTEMBER 7TH

Yesterday we went to Florence, and Antonio joined his regiment. 1000 soldiers are leaving for Albania – not, however, additional troops, but to relieve men returning on leave. Great muddle over getting the troops equipped. Nothing but straw for them to sleep on (the barracks being overcrowded), a shortage of boots and clothes. Crowds of weeping women waiting to say goodbye outside the barracks door.

SEPTEMBER 8TH

Each necessary war-restriction measure is preceded by articles in the daily press, showing that such measures are really conducive to the well-being and comfort of the public. Thus, just before the sale of coffee was forbidden, long medical articles appeared, describing the deleterious effects of coffee on the nerves and constitution: "wine is far less harmful". The meat rationing was preceded by similar articles in praise of vegetarianism; and now the abolition of private cars is accompanied by long articles in praise of bicycling!

SEPTEMBER 9TH

Meanwhile the *mot d'ordre* is optimism, and a complacent calm. The leading article in the *Corriere della Sera* sets the note: "Since the bulletin of the Council of Ministers has expressed, in unequivocal terms, Italy's decision to take no military initiative, the life of the nation has resumed its normal rhythm. The schools will open at their regular date; the farm-work has all the labour that it requires. Commerce and affairs in general have not suffered any serious disturbance. The great transatlantic liners sail as usual from our ports." As to the future: "However this conflict may develop and terminate, it is clear that the last traces of Versailles are wiped out forever. Europe must take a new shape."

These phrases, in slightly different words, are echoed by almost everyone I have met. Many would echo, too, I think, the remark of a Fascist young woman this summer: "A good Italian's duty now is to have <u>no</u> opinions."

Last night the BBC announced the decision of the Cabinet to found its policy on the supposition that war will last three years or more. Here the news is received with incredulity and dismay.

Antonio's half-sister Lily, and her husband, Karl von Hertling (an old cavalry officer) have arrived for a short visit. Both he and his wife, as Bavarian Catholics, are intensely anti-Nazi. They refer to the Brown-shirts as *die braune Affen**, and to Hitler as "the sleep-walker" and "the lunatic". They complain bitterly, too, of the way in which every career – except the army – is closed to everyone who is not a member of the Party. They

---

* The brown apes.

are indignant over the persecution of the Christian churches, both Catholic and Protestant, and speak with great admiration of the Protestant pastors, who, they say, have shown on the whole a greater courage in resisting the régime than the Catholics. Karl, moreover, though not himself free from anti-Jewish prejudice, declares himself horrified by the treatment the Jews have received. After the first pogrom in Munich, he said everyone was ashamed – and when, for a few days, even the bakers were forbidden to supply Jewish customers, the people of Munich (especially the poor) secretly provided them with food. Nevertheless, when I ask him "What proportion of the people you know share your views?" and his wife cries, "Everyone!", he says gravely, "No, no, my dear. You only mean, everyone in our little circle." He goes on to say that in his opinion most of the *pratiquant* Bavarian Catholics, especially those belonging to the aristocracy, and some of the peasants, are hostile to the régime; so are most of the intelligentsia, and in the Army, before the war, about half of the officers – especially the older men. But the great mass of the middle classes (especially the schoolmasters, small officials, government employees, etc.) are quite solidly and uncompromisingly pro-Nazi. So are many of the working men.

They have brought with them their only son, Lupo –
a boy of nineteen, incredibly like Antonio in appearance
and mannerism – but deeply depressed. Once, when we
are alone together, he says to me that his whole life has
been a nightmare, since his parents did not dare to enrol
him in the Hitler Jugend. He is convinced that he will
be killed as soon as he is called up.*

During all the early stages of our conversations
both Karl and his wife were very nervous, keeping
their voices low. "We wouldn't talk like this at home,"
they said, "hardly even in our own house." "Yes, it's
too dangerous," added his wife. "The other day in
Munich I was in a tram, and some people began to say
something against the Führer. I got out at once and
walked home. I wasn't going to run any risk of being
mixed up with them!"

We walk home down the Lungarno in silence.
Suddenly Karl burst out: "But how can people help believing? Day after day, year after year, every paper gives us
the same news, preaches the same doctrine. Plenty of
people say, 'We don't believe what's in the papers: it's all
a pack of lies!' But all the same something sinks in. We're
bewildered; we've got to believe in something…"

---

* Alas, it is only too true. Like many others, he was killed in the war, for a cause
in which he did not believe. [IO, 1980s]

I think of the phrase quoted in Nora Waln's book: *Ein Schlaf-wandelndes Volk*. Wandering now in a nightmare – a nightmare in which we are all caught up.

It is Sunday afternoon. My window looks out over the Lungarno, which is crowded with soldiers. They look just what they are: rough, awkward country boys dressed up in ill-fitting uniforms. One, a little older than the rest, has spent the whole afternoon lying on the strip of grass at the water's edge, playing with his baby daughter and now, as they come back, (the child steadying herself by clutching one of his fingers) I see that he has made her a chain of dandelions. On the pavement, a little further on, a cheap photographer is doing good business. Two gawky, grinning young privates pose for him, leaning against the parapet. Two others, one with his arm around a pretty girl, the other with his mother, are looking at the photographs taken yesterday. *"Sì, è proprio lui!"** A less martial, more homely scene could not be imagined. Then the radio in the room behind me blares out the latest news: bombs falling on Warsaw, refugees escaping. Will these men be taking part in similar scenes?

---

* Yes, that's really him!

SEPTEMBER 11TH

Today the Hertlings have had a wire from home: *Keinerlei Nachrichten.** Their three nephews, all in the army, were called up to their regiments on August 21st and since then they have received no word of news from any of them, not even a field postcard. Yesterday, thinking that perhaps it was the post in Italy that was delayed, they sent a wire to their sister in Germany, to which this is the reply. Moreover, Karl added privately to me that he knew beforehand that the boys would not be allowed to write and that even if one of them should be killed or wounded, his parents would probably not be notified for a long time, nor would they be allowed to wear mourning. After an outburst of rage against the inhumanity of the régime, "It's clear," he added naïvely "that curses don't work, or Hitler would long since be dead."

By the same post they hear from their daughter, begging them to buy her shoes, stockings, gloves, soap and a woollen dress, since she can buy none of these things at home. They assure me that when they left Germany on August 20th no one believed in the

---

* No news.

possibility of war. They thought that Hitler would succeed in obtaining Danzig and the Corridor and were
told that no one would intervene.

SEPTEMBER 16TH

News from Turin indicates the importance attached
to keeping the public calm, even at a risk to their
security. The Prefect of Turin has just been dismissed. His crime is "to have aroused the fears of
the civil population" of Turin and of other towns
near the French frontier by evacuating the schoolchildren and sick people of the region. This he did,
in lack of any official instructions, in the last days of
August, when everyone believed that Italy would be
drawn into the conflict, and it was clear that these
towns were likely to be the first objective of the
French air-force. But now the Prefect is dismissed,
and Starace, having summoned the *gerarchi* of the
district, has made a fine speech, recommending a
resumption of normal life as the first duty of every
citizen.

Here is an illuminating story from Rome, told me
by someone who was present. On the night of August

31st there was a dinner-party and after dinner the assembled guests, gloomy and anxious, were expecting Ciano. When at last he arrived, he was beaming. "You can set your minds at rest," he said. "France and England have accepted the Duce's proposals, France in a spirit of enthusiastic and whole-hearted collaboration, England on general lines; their answers have been communicated to the Führer, and tomorrow morning the news of the general distension will be made public. So go to bed tonight with your minds at rest!" The guests followed his advice, and woke the next morning to the news of the invasion of Poland! Neither the Duce nor his son-in-law were told of it until two hours before the event. Since then the word Axis has practically disappeared from the Italian press.

SEPTEMBER 17TH

Today comes the news of the German ultimatum to Warsaw and that of the Russian invasion of Eastern Poland. Today the sinking of the *Courageous*.

SEPTEMBER 19TH

All the afternoon I have been listening to Hitler's speech at Danzig. It contains, even according to the Italian version of the news, one recognizable lie: the statement that France and Germany had accepted Mussolini's proposal of a peace conference, while England refused it.

SEPTEMBER 24TH

"The Pilot has spoken" – that is the headline that many papers have given today to the Duce's long-awaited speech, of which the first part simply amounts to, "Don't speak to the man at the wheel." The rest is given to an echo of the German thesis that Poland having been "liquidated", Europe is not yet really at war. War can yet be avoided by the realisation that it is "a vain illusion to maintain, or worse still to reconstruct, positions which history and the natural dynamism of peoples have condemned." Italy is to maintain the policy outlined on September 1st: the Italian people are to prepare themselves for any event, to promote every effort for peace, and to work and wait in silence.

For the last week or so the sense of uneasiness and uncertainty has been increasing. From Rome came persistent rumours of the Duce's illness and of the King's threat of abdication. Anti-Fascists spread the news of a military dictatorship. There were speculations about a neutral bloc with the Balkan powers; there was anxiety about Russia. It was repeated that more troops had sailed for Libya and were massed on the Egyptian frontier, and that the air-force, as well as the navy, were still mobilised on a footing of active service. There was more open criticism than has been heard for years (especially in military circles) of the Fascist *gerarchi*. In Antonio's regiment the officers were required to sign a statement that they had taken note of a circular containing the order: "Be silent, and do your duty." Now, with the Duce's speech, there is a sudden détente. In the cafés and in the restaurants that evening, people looked more cheerful; men greeted each other with, "Well, at least we know where we stand!" Once again, one is made aware of Mussolini's immense personal ascendancy.

SEPTEMBER 26TH

I am now in Rome, and have heard from the American Ambassador (William Phillips) about his visit to the King, to bring him Roosevelt's "peace message". As soon as it was cabled to him here, he called upon Ciano and asked him to arrange an interview with the King. Ciano was obstructive; the King was in his fishing lodge, he could probably not be reached for two or three days, and anyway, did Phillips realise that it was quite unprecedented for a message "of a political nature" to be sent directly to a sovereign and not to his Prime Minister? Phillips replied that he was sorry about that, but that he was catching the night-train to Turin. Ciano then said uneasily that he must consult his father-in-law, but reappeared a few minutes later to say, in a more cordial tone, that of course an interview could be arranged the next day. The fishing-lodge, when Phillips reached it, proved to be a dreary little group of *villini* – hardly more than wooden "frame" huts – situated at the end of one of the narrow, bleak and stony valleys of Piemonte, by a rushing torrent. Having lost his way, he arrived late, in a faint drizzle; the gate was opened by a sentry and in the middle of the drive a very small, shabby man in a brown overcoat was standing waiting, quite alone. It was the King. Following him into a bare little sitting-room, furnished in pitch-pine, Phillips democratically remarked how glad he was to have the opportunity of seeing His Majesty under such circumstances and not in a palace. The King's weary, sad little face expanded in a sudden school-boyish grin: "I hate palaces!" The Ambassador then took out Roosevelt's message and read it aloud; the King listened, his face expressionless. When it was finished, he made no comment of any kind; he would hand the message on, he said, to his Ministers. Then rising, "You must remember, Ambassador," he said in a quiet, flat voice, "I'm a constitutional monarch, like the Kings of England and Belgium. I must refer everything to my government." Taking his guest out into the rain again, he proceeded to tell him how many trout he had caught that season and to describe how beautiful the view of the mountains would be, were they not hidden by the mist; he showed great personal cordiality. But of the affairs of Europe he said no single word. Phillips came away with the impression of a tired, sad old man, who had been so often put on the shelf that he had lost the power – perhaps even the will – to affirm himself. On the other hand, the Prince of Piemonte's position is becoming increasingly important. He is now on good terms with the Duce, and has won the respect and liking of the Army.

SEPTEMBER 28TH

A bad day yesterday: the Russo-German "treaty of friendship and interests" and the imposition of the pact on Estonia. Considerable uneasiness and much speculation as to whether, if there is a move towards the Balkans, Italy will be able to keep out. Open speculation, too, as to whether Russia's arrival upon the scene might not be the deciding factor in a change of policy. Meanwhile the tone of the press is still very guarded. Yesterday's *Giornale d'Italia* gives up its front page to a large and dramatic photograph of the Duce piloting a plane (apparently in a whirl-wind), with a quotation from his recent speech: "The Italian people know that they must not disturb the pilot, not continually ask for information about the route."

OCTOBER 3RD

For the last three days no one has spoken of anything but Ciano's journey to Berlin, although no one has any information to go on. But I notice that even the most enthusiastic Fascists are beginning to feel doubtful as to whether any terms that Hitler is likely to propose (even under the moderating influence of Mussolini) could be acceptable to France and England, and even as to whether their acceptance would be conducive to the stable peace of Europe. It is also thought that Mussolini is not likely to weaken his prestige by presenting terms which he knows to be unacceptable.

OCTOBER 7TH

The "peace offensive" has reached its climax. Yesterday I listened to Hitler's speech: the quiet beginning, the hysterical paroxysm of anger during the abuse of Poland, the actor's sob in the throat at the end, describing the horrors of war, following upon peace proposals that cannot be accepted because – apart from everything else – they would not lead to peace.

The first comments of the Italian press are favourable. Hitler's speech is given in full under the headlines, "Hitler reaffirms the German people's will to peace", and the leading article of one important paper begins: "The Führer's has really been a great speech, not only for its convincing clarity but for the sense of deep humanity by which his words are inspired," and concludes with an admonition to the democracies not to allow the few days which will be granted them for "a return to reality" to pass in vain. Private opinion fluctuates, most people intensely disliking the tone of Hitler's speech, but many maintaining that his proposals could and should be considered.

OCTOBER 12TH

Meanwhile an unpleasant feature of the last few weeks – a consequence of the outspoken discontent and false rumours in September – has been a recrudescence of bullying, by the more zealous members of the militia. Yesterday in Florence I found every shop window plastered with little notices, pasted there in the night: *Il Duce ha sempre ragione;** *Il Duce sa tutto, vede tutto, – e ricorda*

---

* The Duce is always right.

tutto.* More directly menacing were other notices in which the *squadristi* declared themselves to be as young, as vigilant, and as ruthless as ever: "The truncheon is not put away for good. Let those who have a bad conscience remember this!" These threats have already, in a considerable number of cases, been carried out. Nor is this the only result of local zeal. The president of a provincial corporation told me that a few days ago he received official instructions saying: "It is inconceivable that a good Fascist should wear the badge of the *Azione Cattolica*. If other forms of persuasion fail, there is always the truncheon." The OVRA too is said to have been very active again, especially in the pursuit of Communists and Masons. In fact the Bogey-Man is with us again – (wearing the face, to Fascists, of a Communist, a Mason or a Jew; to Catholics, of Hitler or Stalin; to Liberals, of a member of the Gestapo or OVRA). And the chief Bogey-Man, Himmler, arrived in Milan yesterday.

OCTOBER 22ND

Yesterday, coming up to Florence in the train, an absurd but characteristic conversation. Having put

---

* The Duce knows everything, sees everything, and remembers everything.

my papers on an unoccupied seat beside me, I moved them as an officer came into the carriage, and in so doing dropped one of them. He bent down to pick it up, and saw its title: *L'Osservatore Romano*. (This is the Vatican paper, whose subscriptions have gone up to four times their original number in the last few weeks, owing to the fact that it is the only paper that prints full and impartial foreign news, although with a strong Catholic bias.) As he gave it back to me he said (using the *voi* which is now declared correct by the régime, instead of the "effeminate" and "foreign" *lei*), *"Ve lo rendo, sebbene sia nemico di questo giornale."** I thanked him, without answering his comment. He was a Colonial officer, carefully modelled on Balbo – the same pointed beard and swaggering, hearty manner. After a minute he leaned across to me. *"Scusate, Signora*, but why do you read this paper?" – "Out of curiosity," I replied, "like other papers." The officer pursed his lips. "But it contains poison – a very subtle poison." An elderly man, sitting in the corner, had put down his paper and was following the conversation with interest. He wore the Fascist badge, but had an intelligent, kindly face. "Sometimes," he now helpfully intervened, with a smile, "a small drop of poison may

---

* I'll give it back, although I'm an enemy of this paper.

act as an inoculation!" But the officer would have none of it. "I dare say. But at this moment, when the whole nation should be *un blocco solo*,* such influences are dangerous – <u>very</u> dangerous, *signora*." And with a last disapproving glance, he went out of the carriage.

I glanced at my other companion, and met his eye; we both shrugged slightly. "He's a *Consigliere Nazionale*," he remarked. Then, reassuringly and paternally, "I shouldn't pay too much attention to what he said." I did not answer, and began to read my book. When I looked up again, my companion had moved a little nearer. "I read it, too," he remarked in a lower voice, jerking his head towards the offending paper, "but in private. If I may offer you some advice, Signora, read it at home!" I nodded. Then I could not resist saying *"C'era di peggio!"*† and, lifting the innocuous *Nazione*, which lay on top of my other papers, showed him the title of the *Daily Telegraph*. He drew back sharply, and returned to his corner seat. There was a long silence; I folded up my papers. Then suddenly, from his corner, my companion spoke again – and in quite a different voice. "A great deal of that poison is needed," he said grimly. I felt very much tempted to reply, but (stories of *agents provocateurs*

---

* One single block.
† There was something worse!

returning to my mind) did not; he felt, no doubt, equally uncertain of me. And so, with alternate glances of mutual suspicion and sympathy, but still in silence, we finished our journey.

OCTOBER 23RD

The evening papers print in italics, with large head-lines, Goebbels' accusation that it was Churchill who ordered the sinking of the *Athenia*. The evidence of two American citizens is given to support the charge, and Churchill is asked how he managed to bribe the previous witnesses. It is difficult to estimate how much ice is cut by such accusations, or by that of England having supplied poison gas to Poland. Today a friend from Rome writes: "England is certainly losing the war of wireless propaganda; it's a pity." But I suspect it's too soon to tell.

NOVEMBER 10TH

I have just been to Rome, to find out whether it was possible to do anything from here about Polish Relief,

either through the International Red Cross or the
Vatican. Both doors were firmly shut: "The Church's
delicate position"... nothing could be done. At last,
however, at the Braccis' I met K., the head of the
Polish colony in Rome. There were three separate
problems, he said: there was the plight of the Poles still
in Poland, there were the great camps of refugees in
Rumania and Hungary, and finally there were a small
number of refugees who had recently reached Italy.
For those in Poland nothing could be done. – "But
the International Red Cross?" – He shook his head.
He had heard only yesterday that the Mission which
was about to start from Geneva had been refused
admission. We all gasped: "But even in Spain..." He
nodded. "You don't understand; the Germans prefer
us to die." Some members of his family had arrived a
few days ago from Warsaw; they had been through the
whole siege. Now 75% of the houses there are unin-
habitable; no pane of glass was left in the town; for
the last days of the siege and immediately afterwards
there had been no light, no water. We asked about the
rumours of plague and cholera, but he denied them.
"But there is some typhoid of course, and cold, and
hunger..." K's face hardened. "I was at the head of the
little deputation of Poles who visited His Holiness last

month," he said. "Perhaps you read in the papers what he said?" "Yes." – "He spoke coldly, <u>prudently</u>. That is not the way to speak to men who…" He broke off. "In any case, as no doubt you know, there is a strong pro-German element in high quarters at the Vatican. Schemes that have been launched have been delayed, frustrated… No, I count on no help from there. There was an ecclesiastic who was talking to me, the other day, about the terrible effects of war upon the human soul. The worst, he said, is the destruction of respect for the Will of God. No, I said, the worst is this: that if, today, I had a chance of shooting down a German woman or child, I would do so without an instant's scruple or pity. That whole race – I no longer feel that they are human beings." There was such complete conviction, such immeasurable bitterness, in his voice that no one answered. (I learned later that he was one of Pilsudski's legionaries, and before that, had been in prison, as a revolutionary, under the Kaiser.)

It was K., returning to our original questions, who broke the silence. The situation of the Polish refugees in Hungary and Rumania, he said, was somewhat different. The suffering was terrible, but help was arriving; there was the British Government Fund, the American Mission, the Quakers… but nothing could be sent from Italy. The government was afraid of its being "misinterpreted"... In the end we discovered that nothing could be done here, except to provide lodging and clothing for the small number of refugees (a few hundred) who have arrived here. It does not seem much...

NOVEMBER 23RD

Last night two young Poles (brother and sister) came to dinner; they had arrived from Warsaw the night before. The sister had been through the whole siege; the brother (a diplomat), after leaving with the diplomatic train had got off it before reaching the frontier, joined the army, fought with it until the end, and then, hiding in ditches, had somehow made his way back to Warsaw, miraculously escaped arrest, found his sister, and succeeded in getting her out of the country with him. Their final departure from Warsaw, indeed, was fairly easy. "They're glad to get rid of us," he remarked, "provided, of course, that we take nothing with us." (They had taken a suitcase each and, out of a large fortune, one hundred marks.) But the journey was nerve-racking, for five different sets of guards came in turn to look at their passports. "Each time," said the girl, "I could hardly breathe."

The stories they told of their experiences were made convincing by a singular lack of personal animosity; they seemed to have gone beyond it. But, "you can't imagine, you can <u>never</u> imagine," the girl went on saying. "Sometimes even I, when I remember, can't believe it's true." She looked in a dazed way round the Embassy drawing room. "And I certainly can't believe that I'm here!" According to their account most of the German officers were very young, and the worst horrors were done by the youngest, mostly when they were either drunk or drugged. "They start taking drugs – mostly cocaine – to keep going," said the brother, adding that he was determined to repeat nothing that he had not actually seen with his own eyes. "Tanks going into action with a Polish prisoner tied to the front, so that we should not shoot: a field in which a peasant, mad with fear, was running round and round under a tree for shelter, while a low-flying plane continued to circle over his head, shooting at him; the machine-gunning of civilian refugees" (not once but several times his sister confirmed, having lain for hours in a ditch while it was going on). "But what I remember best," he added, "is an old peasant and his wife in a little country town, who had come in to market with a load of apples, which the German soldiers promptly seized. The old man was standing by in a passive, despairing state, but his wife went on nagging at him at least to get the apple basket back. So at last he gathered up his courage and, bowing very low: "Of course, of course, they could have the fruit, but would they not be kind enough to return the basket... a poor man's capital... would they kindly understand..." He was taken and shot on the spot, for "insubordination".

They spoke of the siege, confirming other accounts which had reached Italy. They spoke, too, of the German broadcasts on the Warsaw wave-length, which had had so misleading an effect abroad. "But I don't think anyone in Poland was taken in by them," he added. "You see, the Warsaw station signal is a bar of one of Pilsudski's songs, which we all know by heart, and the Germans got one of the notes wrong."

Finally I said: "I want to ask a painful question. Was there great bitterness, at the end, against France and England? Had you expected more effective help?" He hesitated a moment, then answered, "Yes, in the last weeks we felt very bitter. At first, you see, we thought that part of the German army, and especially of their air force, was being kept busy on the Western front; but then, as their reinforcements went on coming, and we heard that nothing at all was happening in the West..." he shrugged – "well, you can imagine what we felt. We had expected to have half the German army to deal with, not the whole. And we <u>could</u> have held out, I swear we could... Of course," he added more quietly, "I know the official explanations. And you must make no mistake, our people do know the truth. After the German occupation, the Germans plastered the walls (those which were still standing) with posters representing a tiny and ignominious figure of Chamberlain looking with shame at the ruins of Warsaw and the inscription: 'Poland, this is what England has done to you!' But the next morning, on each one of those posters, the word England had been deleted and replaced by 'Hitler'!"

1940

Just back from a few days in Rome; not since last
September has the capital been buzzing with so many
contradictory rumours, but extraordinarily little real
information has leaked out. Indeed, each story one
hears is little more than a repetition of the speaker's
personal opinions. Pro-Germans attribute the utmost
significance to the Brenner meetings: "Do you sup-
pose two men like that merely had a quiet talk about
keeping the peace in the Balkans? No – Italy will be in
before May!" Pro-Allies tell long and circumstantial
anecdotes about the violent quarrel that took place in
the Brenner snowstorm: how the two leaders went
at it, hammer and tongs, behind the drawn blinds of
the railway carriage, until the sound of their shouts
drove in Ciano and Ribbentrop to intervene. Then

there are stories about Ribbentrop's Roman visit: how he turned pale – no, was sick – no, fainted, after his interview with the Pope; how he paid a visit of two hours to a Roman princess on the pretext of offering her the Führer's condolences on her husband's death, but really in order to pump her about the attitude of Roman society; how Ribbentrop and his staff all arrived in Rome with large empty trunks, which they took back so heavy with loot – clothes, boots, food – that the porters could not carry them! Much less is said about Sumner Welles' visit. Apparently his interview with Mussolini was hampered by the fact that Mussolini refused to speak either English or French, but used Ciano as an interpreter, thus effectively preventing any spontaneous exchange. Phillips, the American Ambassador, who had not seen Mussolini for nearly a year, said that he appeared to be in perfect health, but heavier and slower, less vital, than before. But as to the substance of the conversation he preserved a discreet ambassadorial silence, merely repeating his previous conviction that Mussolini does not want war if he can avoid it. This is the opinion which it is Ciano's task to promote among the Allies and their sympathizers.

APRIL 8TH

An Italian friend who attended the special performance of the German film of the Polish Campaign has given me an account of it. The Quirinetta theatre – taken by the German Ambassador for the occasion – was filled with a carefully chosen audience: all the principal *gerarchi* (including Ciano, looking very sulky), the German colony and a sprinkling of the more pro-German members of the Roman aristocracy. No diplomats except the Germans, not even the neutrals. Yet even with this audience the film was – as a piece of German propaganda – a failure. Its object had been not to persuade, but to intimidate; over and over again the same note of warning was sounded: this is what happens to those who stand up against Germany! But the lesson – further pointed by propaganda pamphlets sent to the guests beforehand – did not go down well. The first part of the film – showing intransigent Poland, at the instigation of England, preparing for war against a peaceful and conciliatory Germany – was received with bored scepticism; while the "comic" scenes which followed, showing the "decrepit" and ineffectual British ministers, were thought vulgar and boring.

Then the note changed: "Poland has insisted upon war; well, now she shall be shown what it is!" And the rest of the film showed the grim, ruthless destruction of a whole country, a whole people. At the worst moments, though no one dared to comment aloud, a low murmur of disgust spread through the hall – and at the end the guests walked out in grim silence.

APRIL 9TH.

For two days the papers have been filled with attacks on England and the British blockade, and yesterday's evening papers give prominence to "the unjustifiable laying of mines along the Norwegian coast". It is clear that something is brewing, and as I wake up this morning, I find a note from my host on my breakfast tray. "Germany has invaded Denmark at 3 o'clock this morning. German troops have landed at Oslo. Norway is at war." The Italian papers give the same news, but with a wholly pro-German colouring. A few hours later the midday posters state that the Norwegian government, like the Danish, has decided not to resist – her resistance at Oslo being merely, according to Gayda, "a formal gesture, amounting to nothing more than their verbal protest against the English blockade". It is not till this evening that we hear, from the BBC, of King Haakon's resistance, of the British and French promise of help to Norway, and of the sea and air battles.

APRIL 12TH

During the next three days an impartial observer would find it difficult to believe that the Italian press and radio could apply to the same events as the news on the French and English radio. In the Italian papers – so full of compassion, a few weeks ago, for Finland, and of contempt for the Allies' failure to come to her aid – there is no single word of sympathy for Norway. On the contrary, we are given in full the text of the German reproofs against King Haakon's "lack of comprehension" of the friendly, protective intentions of the bombs that were being dropped on him. The British Admiralty bulletins, indeed, are generally quoted, but in small type, while all headlines refer to the German communiqués, which are treated as the only reliable ones.

APRIL 16TH

The anti-British propaganda continues. "I am so afligée by the tone of the radio and the press" writes a woman, once whole-heartedly pro-Fascist, "that it is making me ill. What I have long dreaded is happening; no distinctions are made any longer: the laying of a mine-field is exactly the same as invading a civilized country. It is slavish, our abject echoing of all that horrible doctrine, so at variance with the real Italian spirit." But at the same time she adds: "I do feel that England has a heavy responsibility. So long as the admired and applauded voice is that of Churchill, hectoring the neutrals, breathing fire and slaughter against Germany, and yet letting the really magnificent landing operation take place (magnificent in its execution, odious as it was) one can only feel that something very essential is wrong. Will England *never* arrive in time and save a small country before talking about it?"

The *Giornale d'Italia* publishes on its front page an ingenious little map, depicting the three large gateways at Gibraltar, Suez and the Dardanelles, which "imprison Italy in her own sea"; there are constant jeers (based wholly on the German bulletins) at England's failure either to land in Norway or to score a decisive naval victory and there is even (both in the papers and on the radio) a repetition of the revolting German story that British sailors had machine-gunned drowning German sailors in Narvik bay.

APRIL 18TH

Two very odd days in Rome. We arrive there on a lovely spring morning. In the Villa Borghese Judas trees and wisteria are glowing under the great pines; pretty girls are wearing their new summer dresses; every hotel is packed with visitors. Outwardly Rome has never seemed more beautiful, more prosperous or more gay. But as we drive up to the Excelsior, we get a first slight shock: two German soldiers in uniform – tall, gawky, wooden-faced peasant boys – are standing on the steps. The passers-by stop, stare, nudge each other: "They're from the German military mission" – "Yes, this time they've come without bombs!" – "Nonsense, they're only the grooms of the Horse-show officers".

An underlying current of uneasiness, of discontent, is everywhere. At the hairdresser's I ask for the daily paper. "Here it is, madam; but you'd better hold it with the tongs!" In the cubicle next to mine a Swedish diplomat's wife – oblivious of the fact that voices raised under the dryer carry far – is unbosoming herself to the manicurist. "We're dining tonight at the German Embassy. And perhaps tomorrow I'll wake up to the news that those swine have invaded my country!"

At a large dinner party that night at the American Embassy similar conversations are going on in undertones. "Yes, but the Admiral said to me..." – "Well, but everybody knows that the Navy are the only real fire-eaters! Besides, they're the only people who are ready." "Italian landings in Corfu... Tunis... Dalmatia..." "Twenty-five German divisions at Innsbruck. No, twelve more in Vienna." "What about Croatia?" – "Nothing in it." "Well, I know for a fact that Stojadinović..." "Anfuso sent an official denial to the Ambassador this morning!" "Yes. Quite so. He also sent a similar denial last year forty-eight hours before Albania!" "Anyway, Ciano's rule is over. He'll be sent to take Balbo's place in Libya..." "No, the Viceroy's in Ethiopia... Balbo's too anti-German to be welcome here." "The only hope is the Vatican." "Nonsense, the Pope can't do anything. But the King. The Army would still back him up, if only he'd be firm." "He's too old; he's under the Duce's thumb." "Not at all, it was he who kept us out in September. The Duce's been fuming ever since. For the first time in his life he had to give way, and he hasn't got over it yet." "The Prince of Piemonte..." "My Polish cousin..." "My uncle in Belgrade..." "My brother-in-law in Budapest..." They say, they say, they say... Meanwhile, in the intervals of the anxious, inconclusive chatter, Walt Disney's new film is shown: *Pinocchio.* The audience simulates an unconvincing childishness. "Too enchanting! Don't you adore old Geppetto? And Jiminy Cricket!" – "My congratulations, Mr l'Ambassadeur! A wonderful piece of American propaganda!" And so, still chattering, we make our farewells.

This section of Roman society – the "smart", cosmopolitan world – is mostly anti-German, with the exception, it is rumoured, of a few well-paid informers of the secret police, the OVRA, mostly women. But its reasons for being pro-English – a taste for English country life, English tweeds, guns and riding-boots – are hardly such as to cut much ice with the Duce. Indeed these people, whom he despises, rouse him to his most violent outbursts of rage.

For one thing is certain. Whether the tone of the press is intended to intimidate or bluff the Allies, to reassure Germany, or to arouse the bellicose spirit of the Italian people, there can be no doubt about Mussolini's own attitude. Whatever his sympathies may have been in the past, they are now wholly pro-German.

APRIL 21ST

Popular rumour had fixed upon today – the anniversary of the foundation of Rome – as a decisive date. Indeed an old Tuscan peasant woman, credited with the gift of prophecy, had actually committed herself to three dates:

a) a snowfall on April 10th
b) her own death on April 16th
c) Italy's entry into the war on the 21st

The first two came true, but the third date has brought nothing more exciting than a mild statement by Mussolini that "Work and Arms" must be the slogan of the Italian people.

News from the North, too, is being given a slightly different colour. While there are still jibes at the Allies (as in the now familiar remark that "the democracies, true to their altruistic programme, have decided to fight to the last Norwegian – since now the Poles are wiped out, the Finns exhausted, and the Danes have preferred to stay out") and although prominence and preference is still given in the headlines to the German version of the news, it has been impossible to conceal any longer that Allied troops have landed in Norway, and that a battle is taking place. Now propaganda has taken a slightly different form. "The violence and resolution of the British attack" says the Scandinavian correspondent of *La Nazione*, "show how great a blow the German occupation of Norway has been for England. London has decided to play a decisive card, and her decision to do so must clearly have been taken some time ago, since it is not the gift of the democracies to organize and send off so large an expedition in so short a time." Great prominence is given to the German estimate of British naval losses; the cumulative effect of all this is inevitably considerable, and is now added to by other forms of German propaganda. *Il Tevere*, for instance, is well known to be in the pay of Germany; every railway bookstall has on sale a pamphlet titled "The truth about the *Athenia*" (i.e. the evidence that it was Churchill who sank it); and much popularity is enjoyed by what, at first sight, appears to be an Italian picture-paper titled *Segnale*, which is merely a special edition in Italian of the *Berliner Illustrierte Zeitung* "Signal".

Meanwhile many of the English and Swiss papers (which arrive here freely, but of course several days late) not only report the Italian hostility to the Allies, but attempt to analyse their attitude. The *Daily Telegraph* of April 20th, for example, after commenting on "the insolent, and often menacing, tone of the press", proceeds to contrast it with what is "really" felt and said by the Italian people – and quotes a working-woman saying "give me three *lire* worth of lies" as she buys her paper at a news-stall. Such remarks are, indeed, to be heard on all sides, but to attach any significance to them, even cumulatively, in the sphere of <u>action</u> is, to my mind, an illusion. Such comments, like the anti-Fascists' *bon-mots* which circulate freely (one of the latest is: "What did the 'Fascist martyrs' die for? – For the Cause! – And what shall we die for? – For the Consequences!") are a safety valve: they temporarily relieve the speaker's feelings. But they go no deeper. What <u>is</u> deep – deeper than all dislike of Germany and German methods, than all criticism of present policy and anxiety as to its consequences – is the conviction: "We had no choice." In all conversations with Italians (except for the extreme anti-Fascists) one comes up against the unshakeable conviction that Italy has nothing to hope for from the Allies. This belief, especially with regard to the Mediterranean question, is still the one that awakens the strongest feeling – and that has prompted the rejection of Reynaud's friendly advances.

When however one asks, "But do you really think you will get anything better out of Hitler's victory?" the answer is generally a grim shrug. "We can but try and see." The more extreme Fascists go even further; they admit that Hitler's victory would be temporarily disastrous both to Italy herself and to European civilization. "Perhaps for some years", they say, "we'll be nothing better than a German province." But still, they maintain, Italy must now be on Germany's side, because that – historically speaking – is the side of revolution, of the destruction of the old Europe. Most probably this war – the war to destroy the capitalistic imperialism of England and France – is only a preparation for a second conflict, in which the defeated countries, with Italy at their head, will in their turn revolt against German tyranny, and eventually unite to build up a new European order, in which once again (with both the old tyrannical powers destroyed) words like liberty and civilization may again have a meaning.

In other words, the only glimmer of hope ahead is to be perceived after two wars (one to be fought by themselves, one perhaps by their sons). A grim prospect.

I do not wish to imply that I consider Italy's intervention on the German side as inevitable, but only that the psychological or reasonable arguments against it, produced by optimistic observers, seem to me unconvincing. Military events alone, with their economic consequences, will decide. Had the German invasion in the North indeed been as successful as the German and Italian press claim, Italy might be in by now; a bold and (even temporarily) successful German move in the Balkans might produce the same result. Public opinion is being prepared for it, and I believe that at this moment the country – in spite of all contrary current of feeling – would march. Incontestable Allied successes, and above all, a prolonged demonstration of Allied determination and force – these alone might change the picture. Then, on the crest of the wave, and not now, would friendly approaches by the Allies be timely and effective. But perhaps by then the Allies will not feel inclined to make them. And that, to those who still love the Italian people, and believe in the part they could play in the reconstruction of civilization – that will be Italy's tragedy.

MAY 6TH

After Norway – what? Every country in Europe is waiting. If the Norwegian campaign has not increased the
Italians' liking for Germany, it has certainly increased
their respect and fear. The cult of violence flourishes
on success. So – what next? Switzerland? Holland?
Belgium? Sweden? Rumania? The Caucasus? Every day
brings fresh rumours, and with them the conviction
that Italy too will be in before the end of the month.
The real war is coming.

MAY 10TH

It has come. Belgium and Holland are invaded this
morning. We hear the news by telephone, from the
station-master at Chiusi, our electric light having
broken down so that we have no radio. All the day we
wait for more news: then in the evening a friend arriving from Rome brings some papers. The news is given
without comment; the German, French and English
bulletins are printed. In the evening, the news of the
mobilisation of Switzerland.

MAY 13TH

For the last two days Italians have been trying anxiously to interpret the tone of the press, for a clue as to
what line this country is going to take. For two days
the press and radio have been colourless. The German
version of the Belgian invasion is given in full, but
there is no official comment. The *Osservatore* prints the
Pope's telegrams of condolence to King Leopold and
Queen Wilhelmina, and also an admirable article in
which the facts are clearly and unequivocally set forth.
For forty-eight hours Italian public opinion veers away
from Germany; this, it is felt, is really too much. Then
once again the *mot d'ordre* is given. On Sunday the
12th the principal buildings in Rome are adorned with
large posters, titled "The collapse of the democracies";
the front page of every paper is filled by a full report
of "the iniquities" by the British contraband control;
and today the anti-Allies campaign is in full cry. At the
same time Italians are warned against "an ingenious
renewal" of the feelings of sympathy for Belgium in
1914. The present circumstances, they are instructed, are
entirely different. Belgium and Holland have allowed
themselves to be influenced by "the intrigues of the

plutocratic powers", so that no one can wonder that Germany felt obliged "to remove this last thorn from her side".

In Rome, bands of students "demonstrate" outside the Allied Embassies, and young toughs hang about the news-stalls, to snatch the *Osservatore* from its purchasers. In some cases a regular street fight ensues. A young Fascist, who is heard talking French in Via Veneto with the daughter of a foreign ambassador (they had no other language in common) is hustled off to the *Questura* and deprived of his Party membership card.

I go up to Florence, to see whether it would be advisable for my mother, who is English, to leave. But the advice of both the US and the British embassies is still "No hurry."

MAY 14TH

In Florence the atmosphere is very tense. The papers unite in magnifying every German success; they announce "the annihilation of the Allied air-force, 323 planes destroyed in one day!" The announcement of the fall of Liège and the occupation of Holland is accompanied by long articles on the exploits of the

German parachutists, and hints at further sinister "secret weapons". In town, I find the streets plastered with posters: "England's collapse"; "Woe to those who accept England's help", "Not Hitler, but Churchill, has missed the bus"; etc. The French and English Consulates are both guarded by troops, and as I enter the French Consulate, a procession of students – most of them schoolboys – appear, singing and waving banners inscribed "Down with British piracy". The crowd, however, watches them with an ironic eye. "First they organize a students' demonstration," says a shopkeeper, as we stand in his window looking on, "then they send troops to 'protect' the Consulate from the students; and at 11 o'clock, when it's time for the boys to go back to their classrooms, the troops will be sent home too. *Buffonate!*"* And so indeed it was. One small boy, our doctor's son, was so naïvely unaware of what was required of him that he followed a malicious friend's suggestion and shouted "Long live the holidays!" – was overheard, severely reprimanded, and sent home in tears.

All this is trivial enough, but the underlying uneasiness is deep. The wildest contradictory rumours are spreading.

---

* Tomfoolery!

MAY 15TH

The capitulation of Holland is announced with considerable *Schadenfreude*. On the same day a grocer in Florence receives a letter from a German firm – already offering him Dutch cheeses!

MAY 16TH

The press continues in the same tone. Most significant is Ansaldo's article in the *Telegrafo*. This article, titled *"Problema di Indipendenza"*,* presents Italy's policy today as the logical sequence to the policy pursued in the Risorgimento and the last war. In the Risorgimento Italy – "partly by open warfare, partly by astute diplomatic manoeuvres" achieved her unity; in the last Great War she obtained a frontier on the Alps; now "the time has come to shake off the last yoke, that of the Anglo-French domination of the Mediterranean". This is, to the best of my belief, the only theme likely to awaken genuine enthusiasm. The

---

* A problem of Independence.

German alliance – except to a small circle of *arrivisti** –
will always remain unpopular. But the tradition of
the Risorgimento is in the Italian blood; if they can
be made to see this war as part of the same struggle,
they will fight.

Late in the evening comes the news of the fall of
Louvain and Malines, the occupation of Brussels, and
Gamelin's dramatic proclamation: "The future of our
country as well as that of our allies depends on the
battle which is now taking place... The order is to win
or to die. We must win."

MAY 18TH

We return to the country. None of our peasants are
called up yet. The incredibly beautiful weather, the
fields of ripening wheat, the tulips in the garden, the
woods scented with broom, form an almost unbearable contrast to the turmoil in the mind. The day is
spent in listening to the radio. The Germans have
reached St. Quentin, English and Belgian troops are
still holding on the Schelde, the French on the Oise.
No English papers or letters since the 10th.

---

* Careerists.

William Phillips, arriving on Sunday, is pessimistic about the likelihood of Italy's intervention. A month ago, he says, Ciano told him that the chances of Italy's intervention were 50-50; yesterday he said they were 90%.

A charming story is being told in Rome. Last week the Mother Superior of the Casa della Divina Provvidenza in Turin (Don Bosco's wonderful charity, which cares for over 300 destitute orphans, lunatics, cripples, blind people, etc.) came to Rome, much troubled, to ask the Pope what she should do with her charges in case of war. She was told that His Holiness would not receive her that day, but that meanwhile she could state her problems to one of his secretaries, and was ushered down a long passage into a small, dimly-lit sitting-room. As she sat there, waiting and praying, the door opened and to her stupefaction, the Pope himself entered, alone. She knelt and kissed his ring and then, still confused by his unexpected appearance, and hardly looking up, she told him of her perplexity and distress. When she had finished, he spoke: "Have no fear, my daughter," he said, "Go back to Turin; resume your work there. There will be no war." Without waiting for an answer, he turned and was gone. A few minutes later, having collected herself, the nun was about to get up and leave, when the door again opened and a priest came in, saying that

His Holiness would be able to receive her tomorrow. "But I have seen him!" she cried. "He has just left me!" – "Impossible!" – The priest looked at her as if she had gone mad. The Pope, he said, had spent the last hour in the company of his secretary, in the Vatican gardens. She repeated the conversation. Then the priest took her to a long gallery, in which the walls were hung with the portraits of the more recent Popes. "Look at their faces: whom did you see?" he asked. After a quick glance, "That one" she replied without hesitation. It was Pius X, the simple and saintly Pope whose death, in 1914, was hastened by the outbreak of the last war. The priest nodded; she was not the first, he said, to whom the Pope had appeared in the last few weeks, and always he had brought the same message. The nun returned to Turin, comforted.

MAY 22ND

The Italian press presents the news of the break of the Maginot Line in the most catastrophic light. The Allies' situation is said to be hopeless; Paris and London are described as being "in a state of panic" and British troops as hurrying in "a tragic race towards the Channel".

MAY 23RD

At the same time there is an emphatic re-affirmation of Italy's "solidarity" with the victors. All that is happening, it is maintained, is the fruit of twenty-five years of criminal errors on the part of the democracies. Today, the anniversary of the Italo-German pact, the King presents Goering with the highest Italian honour, the *Collare dell'Annunziata*, which is equivalent to becoming the King's cousin.

How much of all this produces the effect intended it is difficult to judge. Certainly there are dissentient voices. This afternoon we had a refreshing visit from a Colonel – a downright, choleric Romagnolo – who was looking for rooms for his family, in case of war, in Montepulciano. Crippled in the last war, his dislike of all Germans is intense and vehement. "A fine cousin for the King!" he remarks of Goering and *"Raubkrieg"** is his comment on the German successes. All the same, like every other military man, he is impressed by the brilliance and speed of the German tactics, and above all by the sheer quality and quantity of her war material – human and mechanical. "How can any of

---

* Predatory warfare.

us stand up against her?" he asks. "For twenty years all
her energies have gone to nothing else." The thought
of Europe dominated by Germany is repellent to him;
yet he too feels that Italy must come in on her side.
"We have no choice now."

MAY 25TH

The Germans at Boulogne, and advancing towards
Calais.

MAY 26TH

Another official *festa*, for the opening of the men's
club, the *Dopolavoro*. The Prefect comes, the Bishop,
the *Federale*, and about 1000 *dopolavoristi* from all over
the province. There is a children's play, a basket-ball
match, bowls, dancing, a movie… But it is not a festive
occasion. Too much thunder in the air – and anxiety.
The young man who has painted the stage scenery
appears in a resplendent officer's uniform, having
spent the morning in Siena at a meeting of the volunteers for Spain and Africa. Intensely anti-German

himself, like most of the volunteers in Spain, he tells
me that the line taken at the meeting was to diminish
the emphasis on the alliance with Germany. "When
we fight, it will be for ourselves alone, for our full
independence." He does not seem very enthusiastic.
Our local doctor, too, arrives in the deepest gloom,
having just been called up – he is to be sent to Elba;
and the *maresciallo* brings their summons to several
of the peasants.

The news becomes more and more menacing. The
Germans have taken Calais and are moving towards
Dunkirk. The papers proclaim the "desperate plight
of the Allied armies," and repeat, as an acknowledged
fact, the German accusation that Churchill is propos-
ing to sink the *President Roosevelt* in order to bring
America into the war.

We read these papers gloomily in the train, on
our way to Rome. Our fellow travellers seem equally
absorbed in their papers – and equally gloomy.

MAY 27TH

We return to Rome. After dinner we go for a stroll up
Via Veneto and pause to look at the map. Suddenly two

people – a man and a woman – come running up. "Quick, here!" says the man, and produces a bundle of leaflets; from under her coat the woman brings out a pot of paste. In a second the bill is posted up and they have run on; five minutes later the whole street is full of them. They are an appeal, signed by the "Lega Azzurra", to Italians to come and free their brothers of Nice, Tunisia, Malta and Corsica.

MAY 28TH–29TH

Woken by the telephone. It is Mary Senni ringing to tell me of the capitulation of Belgium. She has just heard on the radio Reynaud's announcement and indictment of King Leopold's surrender. The midday "special edition" of the Roman papers gives the same news, but defends the King. He has saved his people from a merciless massacre. The calumniating fury of France and England (Churchill is represented as "foaming at the mouth – a diabolic fury paralyzing his eloquence" *Messaggero*, May 29th) clearly proves the Allies' intention of abandoning the Belgian Army to be massacred to cover their own retreat. The Allied position is depicted as desperate. The German advance represents "a new conquest due to the sublime spirit of self-sacrifice of the army of the

Reich" (*Piccolo*, May 29th), while the Führer is declared
to posses the "martial virtues" and "moral superiority"
of Napoleon (*Lavoro Fascista*).

Most people, on reading all this, seem chiefly to be
puzzled: they don't know what to make of it. But in
general there is approval of Leopold's decision: "Why
should the Belgians let themselves be massacred for
the sake of France and England?" Reynaud's indictment is considered violent and undignified. At the
same time there is a general conviction that this is the
moment that will be chosen for Italy's intervention –
and an uneasy feeling that it is not a very glorious
one. "We'll be sent to kill a dead man" says an officer
uncomfortably. "Jackals, that's what we are turning
into," says my old midwife, adding: "But I'd better shut
up; I'll get sent to the *confino*!"*

In private conversations, too, there is a marked
change of tone since even a fortnight ago. Not only is
everyone profoundly convinced of German invincibil-
ity, but, while there is still a remnant of sentimental
sympathy for France, there is none for England. To the
Fascists she is the personification of all they wish to
destroy; to Liberals, a weak traitor. "It serves England
right" says an old Liberal, once an ardent Anglophile.

---

* I'll be interned.

"For years we've all looked to her as the defender of international justice. And now she's not had the strength to uphold it."

Feeling anxious about my mother's future position here, I try to get some information from the British and American Embassies. By the British, I am told that a veiled warning has been given by the Italians to get British citizens away; by the American, that they received a most definite order from Washington to pack off all Americans on the *Manhattan* on Saturday. At the Swiss legation I succeed in getting a special visa for both my mother and my stepfather, as invalids, to go to a clinic at Valmont; an ambulance carriage is granted by the Red Cross for next Tuesday.

The weekly official publication, *Relazioni Internazionali*, publishes (May 25th) a leading article titled "The decisive hour" which sets forth the official attitude. The approaching German invasion will mark the beginning of total British isolation. Germany is about to achieve her own. "The Italian people will break their chains in the Mediterranean... This is the time for radical solutions, the time to confirm the ideas of Mussolini's revolution; there is no place now for cowards or for those suffering from perennial moral preoccupations. The decisive hour has come."

JUNE 2ND

Last week, while both the English and Swiss radio stated that the negotiations between Sir Wilfred Greene, the British expert, and the Italian experts on the subject of contraband control, had led to "the establishment of a satisfactory basis for negotiation", the Italian press did not even refer to such discussions having taken place. According to the American Ambassador, this is the story of the negotiations:

1) When the discussions between Sir Wilfred Greene and the Italian experts had reached the point of a satisfactory basis, the British expert was told that the matter could not be clinched as Ciano was away in Albania. The British delegation accordingly returned to London where (unwisely) the press made the announcement above mentioned. Whereupon Ciano, returning from Albania, sent for the British Ambassador, informed him that Mussolini was furious over this "breach of confidence" and, on this pretext, broke off the negotiations entirely.

2) Simultaneously François-Poncet, on the behalf of France, had been conveying conciliatory messages to the Duce. France, he said, was now willing to negotiate

on *all* the main points of Italy's claims: Tunisia, Corsica, Djibouti. He was also rebuffed.

3) Finally the American Ambassador, conveying two messages from Roosevelt to Mussolini, went still further in the effort towards conciliation. Already three weeks before he had conveyed a similar message, which had been received by Mussolini pleasantly if noncommittally. On this occasion the Duce had taken some trouble to outline, with moderation and calm, his grievances in the Mediterranean, and his views on "the new map of Europe", which the Ambassador had repeated in full to the President. Now Roosevelt's message went over each of these points, going so far as to promise Mussolini Roosevelt's full support with France and England in the attainment of his objects and guaranteeing Italy (if she refrained from intervention) a place among the Great Powers at the Peace Conference. This communication, which was received by Ciano, met with a curt refusal after a few days. Then Roosevelt followed it up by a second message, this time in a different tone. It contained, thinly veiled, several definite threats: if Italy intervened, her action would change the whole attitude of the US to the present conflict; she would then undoubtedly put all her resources immediately at the

Allies' disposal. This message was met, yesterday, with another rebuff – equally firm in its content and distinctly rude in its wording; moreover it was added that any further attempt at interference on the part of the President would have the opposite effect to that intended.

William Phillips, greatly indignant, now holds the view that all Mussolini's avowed aims have been nothing but pretexts. In the last ten days he has been given the opportunity of achieving them all without bloodshed; and this opportunity he has rejected.

If indeed this is so, the interpretation is not far to seek. Mussolini, profoundly convinced of the inevitable defeat of England and France, is determined to seize this opportunity not only of realizing his original aspirations but of dealing a final and crushing blow to the democracies. He is aiming, not only at new territorial acquisitions, but at a new Europe. If this is so, it is clear that no concessions will be of the slightest use; the only thing that could possibly affect his decision might be an immediate military success of the Allies. Failing that, the date of Italy's intervention can only be a matter of days.

JUNE 3RD

Today the papers are curiously colourless; obviously no further indication is to be given until Mussolini himself announces his intentions. But loudspeakers are being installed in the squares of every town and village.

I spend the day on the telephone, trying to obtain exit visas for my mother and my stepfather Percy, and writing last letters to England.

JUNE 5TH

Our *fattore** receives a telegram from the Siena authorities, instructing him to see that all the rural population be ready to flock to the nearest town or radio as soon as they are summoned. This can only mean a speech of Mussolini's.

JUNE 6TH

Succeed at last in obtaining the visas for my family and they leave at midnight for Switzerland.

---

* Farm manager.

JUNE 7TH

Still no definite news. But the first outward signs of war reach our valley. In the early morning thirty-five bombers heading South fly over us, and in the afternoon about fifty military lorries, bound for the aviation camp at Castiglion del Lago, drive up the road from Rome. The peasants look up as they hear the rumble, say resignedly *Ci siamo** – and get back, while they can, to their hay.

The radio starts atrocity stories about the behaviour of the Allied troops in Belgium, including a detailed story of the "massacre" by French officers of some innocent Italian miners, and the statement that 1500 Belgian refugees have been murdered deliberately by British bombardments on the Belgian frontier. Such stories, however, don't as yet go down well. Even two boys of sixteen and eighteen, who are staying here, merely shrug and say disgustedly: "Who do they expect to believe it?"

---

* This is it.

JUNE 9TH

The German advance on the Somme continues. In spite of a desperate stand, the Germans are rapidly gaining ground, and the Italian papers proclaim that another three days will see the fall of Paris. Meanwhile here we are still waiting. At mid-day, as we are sitting in the garden, comes a telephone message from Montepulciano: posters in the streets announce that today "at a time yet to be stated" the Italian people will hear an important announcement. We hurry to the radio for confirmation, but do not receive it. We wait all the afternoon, and eventually are given a detailed account of the *Giro d'Italia* bicycle race. By now my chief emotion – and I expect that of most other people – is exasperation.

Is it possible to move a country to war, against its historical traditions, against the natural instincts and character of the majority of its inhabitants, and very possibly against its own interests? Apparently it is possible. Today, four weeks after the German invasion of Holland and Belgium, it is evident that it is only a question of days before Italy comes in. In the interval, the nation's mind has been prepared for war. To what extent has this preparation been successful? It is still difficult to say. In a people as profoundly individualistic and sceptical as the Italian, eighteen years of Fascism have not destroyed the critical spirit, and this is allied to an inborn fluidity and adaptability which causes them (now, as in the past) to interpret all general statements and theories in the light of the particular occasion and thus to attach no undue importance (especially where politics are concerned) to abstract formulas or absolute doctrines. Thus most Catholic Italians (though not all) in these last twenty years have not allowed themselves to be unduly dismayed by the abstract claims of the Fascist doctrine that the rights of the State should prevail over those of the Church, but have been content to accept the fact that, in actual practice, it has been easier in the last twenty years than in the fifty years of intense anti-clericalism after 1870, to bring up their children in a Catholic atmosphere at home. They are prepared to yield in principle, where they can gain in practice. And it is this same fluid adaptability (which, to those temperamentally opposed to it, seems a cynical opportunism) that has rendered possible the German alliance. The Axis – regarded purely as a temporary policy of self-interest, forced upon them by the "intransigent" attitude of the democracies – has been accepted by a people which, in accepting it, yet has not modified its instinctive antipathy for Germany, and for the barbaric and brutal

aspects of the German *Weltanschauung*. The only exception to this point of view is to be found in the small group
of young, restless and ambitious professional politicians, *i
gerarchi*, who are out for nothing but an increase of their
own personal power. Arrogant, half-educated (most of
them self-made men), unscrupulous and sometimes corrupt, they represent the worst element in the country,
and are regarded with contempt and disgust by the older
men whom they have superseded and whose ideals they
are betraying. Fascinated by German doctrines of force
and violence and not afflicted, as they boast, by any old-
fashioned scruples, they envisage the increase of German
influence in Italy as likely to bring about an increase in
their own power. It has been they who have been consist-
ently in favour of the Axis and it is they, and they alone,
who want intervention now. But they have youth, energy,
unscrupulousness, on their side, and above all (although
for different reasons) the Duce's support.

What about the rest of the country? One is afraid to
generalize and I can only, of course, speak of the comparatively small number of people with whom I have
been in direct or indirect contact. But one thing has
struck me equally in them all – from the peasant whose
sons have been called up just before the harvest to the
middle-aged officer who fought on the other side in

the last war, from the university professor to the small shopkeeper: a curious, passive fatalism. They don't pretend that they want the war; they freely admit that their admiration for Mussolini in these last nine months has been largely based on their belief in his ability to keep them out of it; yet, now that war is upon them, they are facing the prospect with this strange, melancholy acquiescence. (I must again repeat that I am only speaking of the people I have met; possibly in the industrial towns of the North the mood is entirely different.) It is not exactly patriotism. There is still, it is true, in some a blind, almost religious faith in the intuitions of the Duce. "He has led us wisely for eighteen years," they say, "We can trust him now." They maintain that Mussolini is a match for Hitler; that if he intervenes now, it will be not only to make use of the present chaos to obtain for Italy her independence in the Mediterranean, but eventually, when peace terms are being discussed, to throw in his weight <u>against</u> the establishment of a German hegemony in Europe. A few, too, who have been shocked by the odious tone of the press, feel that it is more decent for Italy to come in, instead of merely yapping at Germany's command. "We'll fight our battles for ourselves." But these are a minority. And under all the talk there is a deep, universal uneasiness.

JUNE 10TH

Well, it has come. In the morning we wake to the news that the Germans are within forty miles of Paris. At midday a telephone message from the *Fascio* of Chianciano orders us to summon all our peasants at 5 p.m. to the *Dopolavoro*, to hear the Duce speak. The radio is not yet installed in the *Dopolavoro* so we put ours in the loggia, and they all gather in the front garden: Antonio and G., S., the *fattore* and the keepers, the school teachers, the household, and about eighty peasants and workmen. *"Attenzione!"* brays the loudspeaker, *"Attenzione!"* I look at the listening faces. Except for a few boys, who think it a lark, they are all grave, expectant, anxious. "At six o'clock the Duce will speak from the balcony of Palazzo Venezia to the assembled Italian people." Then the *"Marcia reale"* and *"Giovinezza"*. Nearly an hour more to wait. The tense faces relax, the crowd breaks up into little groups. The older men stand under the ilex trees, talking in low voices; some settle down on the steps of the loggia, open their baskets, munch a husk of bread, hand around their *fiaschi*; one group sits in a semi-circle on the gravel, playing cards. The radio plays a series of marches and patriotic airs. Antonio, G. and the keepers discuss the young partridges and the

twin calves born that morning: one of them will not live.
I join the teachers; we discuss how many evacuated children we could put up in the school. I go indoors again; a
great bowl of delphinium and lupins take me back for a
moment to an English garden. A whiff of jasmine blows
in at the window. It is all curiously unreal and also <u>boring</u>.
Then again *"Attenzione, attenzione!"* The men rise to their
feet, shuffle closer to the radio. We hear the shouts of the
crowd in Piazza Venezia, the cheering and the bands,
and then (presumably as the scene is relayed to a German
station) a harsh, guttural voice speaking German. At the
incomprehensible sounds the men's faces become blank
and faintly hostile; Antonio makes a joke (I can't hear
what) and they all laugh. Then deafening cheers from the
radio, presumably as the Duce appears on the balcony –
and then his unmistakable voice: *"Combattenti di terra, di
mare, dell'aria,** blackshirts of the revolution and of the
legions, men and women of Italy, of the Empire, and of
Albania, listen. An hour marked by destiny is crossing the
sky of our country: the hour of an irrevocable decision.
The Italian declaration of war has already been handed to
the Ambassadors of Great Britain and France." I look again
at the listening faces. They wear the blank, closed look
that is the peasant's defence. Impossible to tell how much

---

* Combatants on land, sea and in the air.

they have taken in or what they feel – except that it is not enthusiasm. The speech goes on, touching the familiar themes: sanctions, imprisonment in the Mediterranean, war between the poor and the rich peoples, between the young and the decadent. There is the affirmation, too, that Italy has done "all that was possible to prevent the storm". But somehow none of it carries. The speaker's voice is hoarse, strained; the applause, even from Piazza Venezia, sounds forced – very different from that which greeted last year's speeches about Abyssinia or Munich. When at last it is over, there is a silence. Antonio says *"Saluto al Re! Saluto al Duce!"** The men salute automatically, without enthusiasm. Then they shuffle away in silence. We go back into the house and stand looking at each other. "Well, *ci siamo!"†* says Antonio. "I'm going out to look at the wheat." Flatly, gloomily, we go to fetch our hats and coats.

Later in the day, comments are more articulate. *"Macchè*, there won't be a war even now!" declares the cook, Berto, who prides himself on his political acumen. *"Ci sto dietro, io, alla politica."‡* And we discover that to his mind a declaration of war is an open question. "The others won't accept it, and we shall be where we were before."

After dinner we listen gloomily to the radio. F.'s

* Long live the King, long live the Duce!
† This is it!
‡ I follow the political situation.

discomfort has taken the form of saying: "Don't let's listen to England or France. We know what they'll say, and if there was no truth in it we shouldn't care. But now we've *got* to go through with it." But her husband does not agree. "We might as well hear it. *'Le poignard dans le dos** – that's what will be said of us for the next twenty years." So we listen in to both England and France. Duff Cooper's broadcast is shrill, angry, ineffective, and his phrase about "a nation led to destruction by a single bad man" provokes laughter; but Reynaud's short, tragic indictment is unbearably painful: *"C'est l'heure que choisit Mussolini pour nous declarer la guerre! Comment juger cet acte? La France, elle, n'a rien à dire. Le monde, qui nous regarde, jugera."*† We sit in silence, avoiding each other's eyes.

JUNE 12TH

The Germans are encircling Paris. The Italian air force has bombarded Malta; the English Turin, Genoa, and various forts in Libya.

First air-raid alarm in Rome; we hear about it from Serao, for thirty years the legal advisor for the British

---

* A stab in the back.

† It is at this moment that Mussolini chooses to declare war. How to judge this act? France has nothing to say. The world that watches us will judge.

Embassy in Rome and last night one of the very few
to see off Sir Percy Lorraine and his staff. Brought up
in the English legal tradition, passionately Anglophile
and intensely proud of his CBE, the voluble, shrewd,
enthusiastic little lawyer is in a state of deep distress.
"I feel as if the ground is giving way under my feet," he
went on saying. "I still can't believe it. War between
England and Italy! No, anything but that!" Extremely
nervous at first, glancing to see whether both the door
and the windows were shut, and feeling his ground,
Serao loses all caution when he begins to speak about
the Germans. "Barbarians! Traitors!" He tells us how
three weeks ago, on the morning after the first posters
abusing England had appeared in Rome, he was rung
up by the British Ambassador, Sir Percy Lorraine.
"What is the law of your country with regard to the
posting of bills in public places? Isn't government
authorization required?" Poor Serao, shaking in his
shoes and well aware that every telephone is tapped:
"Well, yes, Your Excellency. That, I understand, is
the law, but of course..." – "Will you come round at
once and give me a copy of the relevant passage?" He
hurries round with the required information, to find
the Ambassador very angry. After reading the clear
and unequivocal passage: "Can you explain to me,"

he asks, "why this morning Ciano assured me that the posting of such bills is not illegal?" Serao stammers, "Perhaps some oversight..." "Am I to understand", Sir Percy inquires, "that your Foreign Minister is unacquainted with the laws of his own country?" Then, more quietly, "Well, I shall have to see what my government has to say to this." "At this point," added Serao, "I took my courage in both hands. 'Your Excellency', I begged, 'let me speak not only as your legal advisor, but in the name of thousands of Italians, who are not inimical to England, who do not want this war. These provocations are deliberate. Their object is to force England into a declaration of war. In the name of all the Italians who detest Germany, who still believe that war with England would be a disaster, let me implore you: do not take up these provocations!" The Ambassador smiled. "I daresay you're right", he replied and, added Serao triumphantly, "I believe that in his dispatch my advice was quoted as that of 'a man who has been a good friend to England for many years!'" He shrugged his shoulders sadly. "Well, it's all over now."

In the evening Antonio returns from Rome with the news of an air raid there last night: nothing dropped but propaganda leaflets, but the noise deafening, as the anti-aircraft fire was unceasing, causing the only damage by their own shells, which fell all over the city. Everyone's nerves considerably shaken and the station packed with people leaving. We are applying for twenty evacuated children.

JUNE 15TH

William Phillips has come up from Rome. After a second air raid last night, he does not recommend it to me as the most restful place for my accouchement. His chief occupation this week has been trying to expedite the departure of the British and French Embassies who, four days after leaving Rome, are still stuck at Ancona and Domodossola, waiting for their opposite numbers to leave London and Paris. At last, however, they have got off.

JUNE 18TH

At 5 p.m. yesterday, heard on the Italian radio the news of French capitulation; an hour later, from America, the text of Pétain's dignified and moving broadcast; in the evening, Churchill's brief statement: England will go on fighting. At 10 p.m. a special train passed through Chiusi on its way to Brenner: Mussolini on his way to Hitler, to discuss the terms of capitulation.

JUNE 19TH

Nowhere in the press (except perhaps in an occasional reference to Pétain) can one find any trace of chivalrous feeling, or even of decent commiseration for the vanquished. Today *La Nazione*'s triumphant leading article proclaims that "This is the century of Mussolini and Hitler. From now on, the old continent will begin a new history." The writer foretells "the destruction of an iniquitous slavery," and a return to "the true values of life", while "the old sordid plutocracies bite the dust."

The reaction of our household and peasants is simpler: they are merely joyfully convinced that immediate and total peace lies ahead. "It's all over! Mussolini will get all he wants, without making us fight for it!"

The two leaders drive together through the

beflagged streets of Munich, "a testimony," says *La Nazione*, "even to the most sceptical, that the friendship of these two great men is founded on the Divine Will". Churchill addresses the House of Commons in a speech free from recrimination, but terribly weak in its attempt to explain why so little military help was given to Poland and France. And meanwhile the merciless fighting continues. Strasbourg and Dijon are occupied in the East, Brest and St. Malo in the West, and men continue to be killed – for what?

As, hour after hour, we turn on the radio in hope of news of an armistice, we hardly pay any attention to the news that Russia is occupying Lithuania, Estonia and Latvia. Japan is menacing Indo China. Banditry spreads fast.

JUNE 21ST

Peace terms have been proposed, under terms which enable the victors to enjoy the "full historic savour" of the occasion. The representatives meet in the forest of Compiège, and sign the terms in the railway carriage in which Foch dictated the "humiliating" peace terms of 1918 to Germany.

JUNE 23RD

Here comment on the terms – in private conversation, as opposed to the odious official tone – shows much sympathy for France, as well as shame or at least discomfort for Italy's own role. "Thank heaven, at least, we didn't actually attack France! We didn't deal the death blow!" But for England there is nothing but contempt and hatred. She's considered to have betrayed France, as well as her smaller allies – and is rapidly becoming, in the eyes even of educated and liberal Italians, the sort of monstrous abstraction that Hitler's Germany has become for Englishmen: a personification of powers of evil and retrogression.

JUNE 30TH

Having been seized by labour pains, I hurry down to Chiusi with Antonio to catch a train to Rome. Naturally, the trains are all filled to overflowing with troops, but the kind owner of the station bar, an old friend, attempts to reassure me by pointing out that there is a dining-car on the next train. "If necessary, the baby can be born there." I am not much attracted by this prospect, but agree that it would be preferable to standing in the passage. My baby, however, is considerate enough to delay its arrival and when at last we reach Rome, we are whisked off – in what seems almost embarrassing comfort and splendour – in the American Embassy car to the beautiful house and solicitous care of my kind godfather William Phillips who, though his wife and staff have already left, is still waiting for orders from Washington to go home himself.

We see many friends – all very depressed, mostly hating the intervention. But much criticism of England everywhere, even among the most anti-German.

JULY 3RD

My first air raid last night. The sirens began just after midnight; I was still awake and was joined by William Phillips. We sat talking pleasantly in the dark for about one hour, heard one distant burst of fire and then the all-clear signal. Altogether a singularly *unalarming* experience, except apparently to the lions in the Zoo, who went on roaring all night. But, as the first wail of the sirens was heard, my thoughts went to England and France.

JULY 6TH

This is a strange period of waiting. The Roman summer, with the city half empty and the black-out at night, is more beautiful than I have ever seen it. In the evenings we dine out under the ilex trees of Villa Taverna, shimmering with fireflies.

JULY 7TH

I have just seen the Italian version of the UFA documentary film *La Battaglia della Manica*. It is a terrible document and also, to judge by the reaction of the Roman audience, a most effective piece of propaganda. The object, throughout, is to present an overwhelming spectacle of force. We see picture after picture of the German advance; and, finally, German troops marching down the Champs Elysées to the Arc de Triomphe, preceded by a brief glimpse of the Allied troops, headed by the Grenadier Guards, parading before Foch in 1918. "That was the past; this is today – and the future."

("Nous sommes l'Empire à la fin de la décadence
Qui regarde passer les grands barbares blancs!")*

Whereas the German film of the invasion of Poland had only been shown, three months ago, to a carefully selected audience, which received it with coldness or disgust, this film is packing the largest cinema in town. There was silence, indeed, and an occasional gasp, at the sight of the destruction of Rouen and Dunkirk, but there was also a good deal of applause: applause for Hitler reviewing his troops, applause for the entry into Paris, applause even for the German flag flying over Versailles.

JULY 8TH

The return of 700 members of the Italian colony in England, with the Italian Ambassador Bastianini, has given rise to a fresh outburst in the press against "revolting instances of British brutality". The papers report stories of priests and nuns insulted and flung into prison, of large numbers of women and children imprisoned. Moreover the returning travellers give a heated account of the filthiness of their ship, the *Monarch of Bermuda*

---

* I am the Empire in the last of its decline,
  That sees the tall, fair-haired Barbarians pass!

(which apparently had just been used as a troop ship and not been cleaned), of the two days which they were obliged to spend below deck at Glasgow, with all the portholes closed, of the lack of water and bad food, and of the deliberate rudeness of police, porters and stewards. During the last days in London many of the Italian colony, including my physician Castellani, found it necessary to sleep in improvised dormitories in the Embassy to escape arrest, and the last unfortunate Italians in the provinces had no means of escaping from the general fifth column hysteria. All this, of course, has been greatly magnified by the press, but even Castellani, with pro-English sympathies and certainly not fussy about comfort, admitted that treatment in London and accommodation provided on board was quite unnecessarily unpleasant – and in marked contrast to the excellent treatment received by the British diplomats on the *Conte Rosso*.

JULY 15TH

I have seen today a Swedish friend who has just been in prison in Florence for a fortnight for "imprudent speaking" and is now expelled from the country. She has lived and worked in Florence as a Swedish masseuse for thirty years. Undoubtedly she has not been prudent in her frank expression of anti-German feeling, although the actual remark which caused her arrest was nothing more than the expression of a hope that her country would not soon suffer the same fate as Norway. She was fetched by the police at 10 p.m., allowed to take nothing with her but the clothes on her back and ninety lire in her purse, and taken to the common women's prison of S. Verdiana. Here she spent three nights in a tiny cell, together with a Russian woman suspected of espionage, and then was moved to a large dormitory which she shared with forty-seven other political prisoners – mostly English, a few French and one Swiss girl. None were allowed any visitors, to write any letters or to have any books. The beds were infested by bugs, the lavatories approximately clean. The food, unless eked out by what the prisoners could buy for themselves, was very poor and scanty, the manners of the nuns very harsh. After a fortnight most of the French and English were let out, and our Swedish friend at the same time, with the proviso that she must leave the country immediately. She is now waiting for the German transit visa, to return home.

JULY 16TH

A lunch party to meet Bastianini, the Italian ambassador in London. Dark, thin, nervous, indisputably able, a certain charm of manner – "l'homme arrivé" (with a sleek, elegant little wife, once a typist of Perugia) – he is considered one of the "coming men" of the régime. I didn't like him – I think chiefly because his conversation, although intelligent, was tarred with contempt – the contempt of the new world for the old, of the self-made man for those who have attained with ease what he has achieved with effort. Speaking of the future, he was entirely prepared to envisage the complete domination of Europe by Germany. Italy should again become, in his opinion, a tourist country, attracting the money of all the pleasure-seekers of the world. As to the Italian people: *"Non troppa libertà,"** – he apparently considers there is still too much. "Too many ideas, too much initiative, are dangerous for a people." The successful revolutionary is turning into a Tory. As for England, he was only there for three months, at an extremely difficult time; but it was impossible not to feel that there too a preconceived

---

* Not too much freedom

resentment had falsified his perceptions. His readiness to see a slight where none was intended, his determined generalizations about British decadence and incapacity for self-sacrifice (as exemplified, for instance, by the persistence of the English week-end habit!) – all these suggested an individual class hatred, as well as national prejudice. The English, he maintained, are done for because their character is now hopelessly rotten; all that is left is corrupt and sterile. *L'Inghilterra è finita.**

It is hardly possible to overstate how universally this opinion is now held here. Daily the press and radio insistently proclaim the inevitability and immediacy of the destruction of England, her incapacity to defend herself, her lack of trained men, of munitions, of food. Churchill's speeches are considered vain boasts, based on no foundation of fact – a cynical last attempt to bolster up the English people to meet their inevitable destruction. At the German Embassy in Rome, it is said, there are both optimists and pessimists. The optimists say that the war will be over in mid-August; the pessimists, in September.

---

* England is done for.

JULY 17TH

Meanwhile the lull continues, the long-expected German invasion has not taken place. Every kind of rumour has sprung up again. A friend, from her castle at Palestrina, sends a note imploring me to go out there at once for the baby's birth; she knows "for certain" that there is to be a bad bombardment of Rome tomorrow night, synchronizing with the beginning of the German invasion of England. So it goes on. Every night I listen to the BBC trying to form a picture of what is *really* happening in England, but it is unsatisfactory, baffling. All letters from England are a month old. What is happening? What can be happening?

JULY 20TH

Last night Hitler's speech. It is received here with almost universal approval; even those people who are not admirers of Nazism consider it a genuine effort towards peace and a last chance for England to save herself from destruction. That this destruction will be inevitable and will be swift, if Hitler does attempt it, no one doubts.

JULY 23RD

Last night Lord Halifax's speech, removing any last doubt as to how England has received Hitler's proposals. We sat in the American Embassy listening to it gloomily on the American radio: two Italians, one Belgian, three Americans. At the end: "Do you think the door to peace is still open?" asked one of the Italians. "Shut and barred," said the other.

This diary was interrupted at this point by the birth of my daughter on August 1st. In the autumn I decided, having a wonderful Swiss nanny to help me with my baby, that inaction was no longer bearable. Surely there must be some work, directed towards the relief of suffering rather than any war aim, which even I, an Anglo-American and a non-Fascist, could find to do? In the autumn of 1940 I began to work in the Prisoner's Branch of the Italian Red Cross – and until the spring of 1943 had no more time for writing.

Afterword

Iris Origo's handwriting was famously illegible. When family, friends and publishers despaired of deciphering her letters, manuscripts or notes, the experts would be called in. They included her daughters Benedetta and Donata, her long-suffering secretary and her publisher and close friend Jock Murray, who claimed to have mastered a special technique for reading Iris Origo. He loved to repeat the story of how, on his return to the office after a day in Manchester, he found the entire staff poring over a long letter from Iris. All had been – more or less – deciphered save the last sentence. He took the letter home with him. "The trick," he said, "is to have the page at eye level, so I had a bath and a snifter, as Osbert [Lancaster] used to call it, and crept past the table on all fours. It read: 'Dearest Jock, I can't read what I have written. Please type it out and send a copy to me.'"

So when a search for family photographs unexpect-edly yielded a promising-looking brown box bearing the legend "Unpublished" in my grandmother's familiar scrawl, I sent up a quick prayer for typewritten material. The brown box turned out to contain many folders of varying dimensions, mostly almost identical versions of standard typewritten pages untidily stapled together, some of them bearing the title "Italian Journal, 1940". Unpublished – but not unknown to scholars of Iris Origo's work, among them her son-in-law Giangiacomo Migone and her biographer Caroline Moorehead. Iris Origo herself quoted these papers in her autobiography *Images and Shadows* and refers to them in her best-known work, *War in Val d'Orcia*.

Why then was this journal never published? Originally it was not meant to be, I believe, being a very private record in which Iris could give voice to thoughts and feelings she was usually forced to suppress, an occasion to reflect on the extraordinary events to which she was witness and could only discuss with her husband and a handful of friends. Iris was good at keeping her mouth shut and her ears open – she knew how to draw people out with a few strategic questions and her keen powers of observation never deserted her, not even when her sentiments were fully engaged and her sense of justice outraged.

Initially she did not intend *any* part of her diaries to be published. *War in Val d'Orcia* was not meant for the public either, yet was published by Jonathan Cape in 1947, shortly after the end of the conflict. Iris was persuaded to take this step because she strongly believed the rest of the world should hear the other side of the story – how ordinary Italians in a remote Tuscan valley suffered the consequences of war and did not hesitate to rescue and shelter their fellow human beings at great personal risk. She must have considered her pre-war journal to be of little interest to others when set against these world-shattering events. Yet in the eighties she showed it to her son-in-law Giangiacomo Migone (husband of her daughter Donata), along with a short piece describing a trip to Libya in 1939 with her husband, Antonio. Migone, who in 1984 founded *L'Indice dei Libri del Mese*, Italy's most prestigious literary review to date, immediately recognized the value of both works and encouraged Iris to re-read and set them in order. But as Iris's health declined, she put aside all revision. Almost immediately after her death in June 1988, *L'Indice dei Libri* published her Libyan piece (translated into Italian by Iris herself) on the Italian agricultural settlements established by Mussolini on land confiscated from the Bedouin. The publication of the pre-war journal was put off to a later date, and then never took place.

In my memories, my grandmother – Nonna, as her many grandchildren called her – has a pen close to hand, usually a leaky ballpoint that left stains on armchairs, chaises-longues and quilted satin counterpanes, which gave away her favourite writing haunts. At La Foce she wrote in her little study on the upper floor, which had much the best view of the Italianate garden, with Pinsent's deceptively simple box-hedge geometries laid out at a glance. The delicately painted bookshelves were crammed to overflowing and every surface, even the window-seat cushions in leaf-patterned sea-green and white cretonne, was obscured by stacks of books of all shapes and sizes. There barely seemed to be room on her desk for her typewriter amidst much-thumbed paperbacks, huge dusty tomes, the odd garden catalogue and typewritten sheets of paper covered in a flurry of scribbles, scratched-out words and strips of paper ineptly glued on and curling at the edges. Research was fundamental and Iris would never shirk hours of painstaking labour simply because they yielded only a few extra words. She prided herself on being a historian and her best biographies draw on new material gleaned from archives and unpublished collections of family letters and documents (*Leopardi*, *The Merchant of Prato*, *The Last Attachment*).

As a child, I was encouraged to write for her and presented her regularly with poems and short stories. Despite their obvious shortcomings I can't recall a single word of criticism, only unconditional approval. It was never her way to correct or proffer advice – when pressed, if she deemed the author's age adequate to withstand any implied criticism, she would only say: read it through. The more you read it through, the more you will want to leave out. If the price to be paid for all these deletions and afterthoughts was a supremely untidy manuscript, so be it. This being her philosophy, I can well imagine her irritation when her step-father, the literary critic Percy Lubbock, asked to explain the pristine condition of his drafts, said: "I think *before* I write."

Iris was brought to Italy in 1911, at the age of nine, by her English mother, Sybil Cutting. Her American father, Bayard Cutting, who died of tuberculosis when he was only thirty, had expressed the wish that his only child be brought up abroad. But her immensely wealthy American grandparents were opposed to Iris's going far away and a bitter war over who should have the final say in deciding her upbringing and education was waged on both sides of the Atlantic. Finally Sybil, availing herself of her status as sole surviving parent (though a more unmotherly figure is hard to imagine) got her way. Iris grew up in the privileged atmosphere of expatriate Florence and the splendid setting of Villa Medici on the Fiesole hill, where the flower of Tuscan humanists once gathered around Lorenzo the Magnificent. Iris was introduced to the wonders of Renaissance art by their neighbour Bernard Berenson. Edith Wharton, Henry James, Aldous Huxley and Somerset Maugham met in her mother's literary salon, where architects Geoffrey Scott and Cecil Pinsent discussed their designs for Italianate gardens commissioned by Florence's foreign community. However, Iris was a lonely little girl, who rarely had a chance to emerge from her ivory tower. Then in 1917 came the Italian army's shattering defeat at Caporetto and an endless stream of refugees. "The face of humanity in flight" produced an everlasting impression on fifteen-year-old Iris. But apart from these brushes with reality, the young Iris had little chance to mix with Italians and observe the Italian way of life – until she met her future husband, an Italian aristocrat called Antonio Origo.

On a blustery October day in 1924 Iris and Antonio, soon to be married, fell in love with a spectacularly wild and desolate valley in southern Tuscany, the Val d'Orcia, and with a half-ruined fifteenth-century villa at the heart of a large estate named La Foce. They dreamed of turning the arid clay hills, where only wild broom blossomed, into fertile pastures and rippling wheat-fields, neatly groomed olive groves and new vineyards. They imagined bringing roads and schools and medical care to the destitute, largely illiterate farmers of the Val d'Orcia. La Foce and its people would become a shining example of bucolic peace and prosperity, the revival of an ideal community from a classical Golden Age.

Extraordinary as it may seem, their vision came true. Between 1925 and the start of the Second World War, La Foce became the heart of a land reclamation project of truly epic proportions. Faced with the gargantuan task of bringing a forgotten valley back to life, Antonio and Iris laid out a pragmatic plan of action based on a profoundly romantic vision: "Neglect, indigence and suspense are etched on the faces of men and the earth alike. We heard the plea, measured our strength and decided." The fact that Antonio, not Iris, wrote these words, gives us the measure of their unity of purpose and ideals. To the dismay and incomprehension of family and friends, they proceeded to invest all their capital and energies in La Foce, helped by incentives and loans provided by the Fascist government, in which agricultural policy played a major role.

But then their only son Gianni died suddenly, aged seven, of tubercular meningitis. By a terrible coincidence, Gianni was the same age as Iris herself when she lost her father. Many marriages do not survive the death of a child and Antonio and Iris Origo struggled desperately to adjust, in their very different ways. Iris turned to her books and her writing and her friendships in England, where she came into contact with a world far removed from the practical agricultural and social problems of the Val d'Orcia or the political gossip of the Roman aristocratic salons. In London she visited Virginia and Leonard Woolf, attended pacifist rallies to hear Max Plowman speak and supported Lilian Bowes Lyon in her efforts to bring Jewish children to safety under the Kindertransport scheme. Back at La Foce, Antonio buried himself in agricultural work. Their marriage did not end, but they spent long periods of time apart and led separate lives. Yet Iris never entirely abandoned La Foce, coming back at regular intervals. In 1938 she took the momentous decision to return permanently and make it her home again, at the side of her Italian husband.

Readers will ask why Iris almost never mentions my grandfather in any of her books. The answer lies, I believe, in both Antonio and Iris's fundamental belief in safeguarding their privacy. Though immensely proud of his wife's writing, Antonio would never have sanctioned any speculation about his personal sentiments and loyalties, his role as President of the *Consorzio della Bonifica* (the Fascist Consortium for land reclamation) or his growing feelings of shame and betrayal caused by the behaviour of his King and the Fascist government. Antonio set great store by bravery (he was awarded the Silver Medal of Military Valour during the First World War, bestowed on him by the Duke of Aosta, the only other man who could match his height of six-foot-five) and was a natural leader: his authority saw La Foce through many a difficult situation during the German retreat through Tuscany in 1944. Fluent in four languages, he could meet German officers on their own ground, negotiate with partisans (who offered many varieties of political creed and honesty) and reassure anguished peasants, all with the same ease. At the same time, he was a cultivated man who grew up in a house where the arts held sway. His mother was a singer and his father, the marchese Clemente Origo, was a talented sculptor and painter. Clemente's great friend was the poet Gabriele d'Annunzio, lyrical visionary, bloodthirsty glorifier of war, decadent aesthete and dandy: Antonio's childhood must have been filled with people striking virile poses and declaiming patriotic verse. Possibly as a reaction, he chose to make his feelings less evident and preferred action to rhetoric, just as he preferred the wild beauty of the Val d'Orcia to frequenting aristocratic circles (on escaping tea at La Foce with the exiled Queen of Greece, he is said to have muttered: "They are unbearable, these unemployed queens"). Iris, though a true intellectual, was undoubtedly fascinated by his pragmatism and could not resist the opportunity to put her own ideals into practice at his side.

On her definitive return to Italy in 1938, Iris had to face the changes her adopted country had undergone. She herself tells us, with some embarrassment, that as a young wife she was completely taken up with her personal concerns and oddly detached from events in Italian political life. The effort of passing from the cosmopolitan self-absorption of the Villa Medici to life on a Tuscan farm and her new role as wife and mother meant that the rise of the new Fascist regime went largely unheeded by her. Despite an instinctive dislike for those aspects of Fascism that it was impossible to ignore in everyday life, Iris remained for a long time very conscious of her foreign origins and reluctant to criticize events she felt she could not fully understand.

Her feeling of being considered an outsider was

certainly justified. My grandfather had access by birth to the stifling, closed circle of the few Roman aristocratic families that mattered and they undoubtedly looked critically on his reserved, blue-stocking wife, who spoke too quickly and could not pronounce her Rs. Throughout her life Iris put up with a certain amount of distrust and antagonism from a large slice of the Italian intelligentsia. Though revered intellectuals and antifascists such as Silone, Salvemini and Umberto Morra were close friends and praised her work in glowing terms, her gender, wealth and nationality counted against her in some Italian circles. She could never quite rid herself of the aura of the wealthy foreigner, whose marriage to an Italian nobleman did not entitle her to write of Italian history and literature. On the other hand, the farmers and workers on the estate at La Foce did not quite know what to make of the elegant, aloof lady who showed them such generosity and compassion. Florence, accustomed to eccentric expats and their literary salons, was more welcoming, but there Iris was uncomfortably close to Sybil Cutting and her backbiting, idiosyncratic coterie. This sense of rootlessness, of never totally belonging to a single place or culture – dating back to the very different family influences of her childhood and the cosmopolitan upbringing her father wished for her – was a leitmotif in my grandmother's life, and one that she explored in her autobiography, *Images and Shadows*.

I remember my teenage self being irritated by her relentless interrogations on this very subject. Did I feel more Italian or English? And how much did I identify with the background of my Argentinian father, with his Ukrainian roots? As the eldest grandchild, I spent a lot of time with my grandmother and received a great deal of attention from her. My father, a concert violinist, was often away on tour, and my mother sometimes accompanied him in the early years of their marriage. I was judged old enough to be left with Nonna, who read to me, drew up lists of books she thought I would enjoy (I do not remember her ever getting one wrong) and passed on to me in my earliest years her distinctive inability to pronounce her Rs. After me came six other grandchildren and Iris rediscovered the joy of having small children around her again, writing that "my grandchildren have bestowed upon me the happiest hours of my old age". She organized picnic parties, charades and plays and, above all, she read to us. In the flickering firelight of the library, which never quite reached its darkest corners, her rendering of *The Black Ribbon*, the family ghost story passed down by her Irish ancestors, caused each one of us to dread bedtime, with the barefoot rush down the smooth terracotta-tiled passage to the safety of our rooms and blankets pulled over our ears.

The rite of passage for us all was when Nonna pulled out her dreaded "Gianni book", as we called it, the heartbreaking account of her only son's short life, complete with photographs of him at all ages and even – which was when our sobs, bravely held back till then, inevitably broke out – on his deathbed, surrounded by Madonna lilies.

The name Iris Origo is linked, in most people's minds, to a definite time and place. She is best known for *War in Val d'Orcia: An Italian War Diary 1943–1944*, a terse, compelling account of how a small rural community in Tuscany survived the horrors of war. Iris and Antonio are committed to protecting the farmers who live on the estate of La Foce and the twenty-eight refugee children entrusted to their care. But soon they find they are unable to deny the same help to the "unending stream of human suffering" that washes up at their door day after day: runaway Allied prisoners of war, deserters from Mussolini's army, ex-Fascist officials, partisans hiding in the woods and townspeople fleeing bombs and hunger. As the fighting moves nearer and Nazi paratroopers take over La Foce, the Origos find themselves on the front line. They must flee on foot, leading a group of sixty people (including four babies and twenty-eight children) through eight miles of mined fields strafed by Allied planes to the relative safety of Montepulciano.

A Chill in the Air: An Italian War Diary 1939–1940 is very different in content. Just as *War in Val d'Orcia* is the story of La Foce during the final epilogue (for Italy) of the world conflict, *A Chill in the Air* reflects the increasingly oppressive atmosphere of a country on the brink of a war for which it is entirely unprepared. Iris Origo's account of those years makes compelling reading. She pores over the Italian newspapers and reflects poignantly on the changed attitude of her adopted country towards her beloved England, all the while holding our interest with an effortless flow of anecdotes, chilling wartime jokes and insider accounts of diplomatic negotiations doomed to failure. Her shrewd political analyses are backed and illustrated by a wealth of detail drawn from a great variety of social and political backgrounds. Conversations with major political figures, confidential information from friends in diplomatic and military circles and the despairing predictions of her anti-Fascist liberal and Catholic neighbours at La Foce are vividly recounted in these pages and Iris excels in bringing to life the prevailing atmosphere of uncertainty and unease. She records the puzzled, aggressive or cynical reactions in the towns and in the countryside as Italians from all walks of life – and she counts herself among them – struggle to understand the fate of their country. As a uniquely placed observer who can claim a profound knowledge of Italy and things Italian, Iris has access to many different voices. *A Chill in the Air* is set mostly in Tuscany and Rome where Iris Origo's godfather, William Phillips, was the American Ambassador. Iris counted many diplomats, intellectuals and liberal politicians of different nationalities among her friends and acquaintances, and through her husband Antonio she met the leading members of the Roman aristocracy, many of whom frequented the King's and Mussolini's inner circles. Yet Iris also records the voices of shopkeepers and artisans, and especially those of the peasants and workmen at La Foce, who turn to the Origos for advice and a word of hope.

As always, Iris keeps her private life out of these pages – to the point that we learn that she is expecting a baby only when the American Ambassador voices a doubt whether Rome, where the first air raids have begun, is the ideal place for an accouchement. Iris is adept at concealing her personal emotions, though this in no way detracts from her capacity to suffer with the victims of war and injustice. A recurring note is her frustration that, as an Anglo-American, she is barred from any contribution to war work – she feels so useless that it even takes some of the joy out of her pregnancy, long-desired and unexpected (Iris was thirty-eight, old for child-bearing in those times). Her need was always to take action, to make a difference. Deep down, though she was herself a true intellectual, she believed that a life entirely dedicated to contemplation and intellectual pursuits was selfish and fruitless.

A Chill in the Air ends abruptly in July 1940, a few days before the birth of her daughter Benedetta. Shortly afterwards, Iris finally finds work with the Red Cross, which absorbs her so completely that she concludes her diary in a brief sentence – "and until the spring of 1943 I had no more time for writing". The reader is left hanging as Iris embarks on the life of action she set such store by. Three years later, when she picks up the thread of the narrative again in *War in Val d'Orcia*, the tale she has to tell is very different.

Katia Lysy

PUSHKIN PRESS

Pushkin Press was founded in 1997, and publishes novels, essays, memoirs, children's books—everything from timeless classics to the urgent and contemporary.

Our books represent exciting, high-quality writing from around the world: we publish some of the twentieth century's most widely acclaimed, brilliant authors such as Stefan Zweig, Marcel Aymé, Teffi, Antal Szerb, Gaito Gazdanov and Yasushi Inoue, as well as compelling and award-winning contemporary writers, including Andrés Neuman, Edith Pearlman, Eka Kurniawan, Ayelet Gundar-Goshen and Chigozie Obioma.

Pushkin Press publishes the world's best stories, to be read and read again. To discover more, visit www.pushkinpress.com.

═══

THE SPECTRE OF ALEXANDER WOLF
GAITO GAZDANOV

'A mesmerising work of literature' Antony Beevor

SUMMER BEFORE THE DARK
VOLKER WEIDERMANN

'For such a slim book to convey with such poignancy the extinction of a generation of "Great Europeans" is a triumph' *Sunday Telegraph*

MESSAGES FROM A LOST WORLD
STEFAN ZWEIG

'At a time of monetary crisis and political disorder... Zweig's celebration of the brotherhood of peoples reminds us that there is another way' *The Nation*

THE EVENINGS
GERARD REVE

'Not only a masterpiece but a cornerstone manqué of modern European literature' Tim Parks, *Guardian*

BINOCULAR VISION
EDITH PEARLMAN

'A genius of the short story' Mark Lawson, *Guardian*

IN THE BEGINNING WAS THE SEA
TOMÁS GONZÁLEZ

'Smoothly intriguing narrative, with its touches of sinister,
Patricia Highsmith-like menace' *Irish Times*

BEWARE OF PITY
STEFAN ZWEIG

'Zweig's fictional masterpiece' *Guardian*

THE ENCOUNTER
PETRU POPESCU

'A book that suggests new ways of looking at the world
and our place within it' *Sunday Telegraph*

WAKE UP, SIR!
JONATHAN AMES

'The novel is extremely funny but it is also sad and
poignant, and almost incredibly clever' *Guardian*

THE WORLD OF YESTERDAY
STEFAN ZWEIG

'*The World of Yesterday* is one of the greatest memoirs of the twentieth
century, as perfect in its evocation of the world Zweig loved, as it is
in its portrayal of how that world was destroyed' David Hare

WAKING LIONS
AYELET GUNDAR-GOSHEN

'A literary thriller that is used as a vehicle to explore big
moral issues. I loved everything about it' *Daily Mail*

FOR A LITTLE WHILE
RICK BASS

'Bass is, hands down, a master of the short form, creating in a few pages
a natural world of mythic proportions' *New York Times Book Review*